TWO SIDES OF THE MOUNTAIN

The Holy Conversation

by

James E. Morel

TWO SIDES OF THE MOUNTAIN

Paperback ISBN: 978-1-949021-19-6
eBook ISBN: 978-1-949021-20-2

Printed in the United States of America

DEDICATION

I must begin by dedicating this book to the purposes of God in the earth today. For however He may desire to use this work, I pray that He may be glorified in and through it. I must continue to thank my biggest supporter, my wife Pamela, who has always walked side by side with me in all the endeavors I have undertaken throughout our forty-seven years of marriage. Finally I thank all those in the church that I serve as pastor in New Hampshire who have encouraged me to continue writing, especially Janet Gilman, a true and faithful servant of our Lord.

CONTENTS

Introduction

IN MY EXPERIENCE AS a pastor, I have found that many Christians walk about with no more hope or vision for this life than those who are not Christians. I have a deep conviction that this should not be the case. Jesus said in John 10:10, "I have come that they may have life, and that they may have it more abundantly." The abundant life is His desire for all Christians. For the vast majority who do not enjoy this abundant life, there remains the question of how one acquires it. Jesus does not leave us to grope in darkness hoping to stumble upon the reality of His promises. He tells us exactly how to acquire this life and where it is found. Colossians 3:1-3, tells us plainly, "If then you were raised with Christ, seek those things which are above, where Christ is, sitting at the right hand of God. Set your mind on the things above, not on things on the earth. For you died and your life is hidden with Christ in God." Our destiny is to be found in Him. He is the author and perfecter of our faith (Hebrews 12:2). We are to live and move and have our being in Him (Acts 17:28).

Dreams Formed in Christ
Since man is prone to dream his dreams,
to look beyond the here and now,
to conjure with his mind,
the things that he would do and be,
then let my dreams be formed in You.
I say, then let this be,
for I, being me, cannot reach to heights
wherein you dwell,
I can only ask that I might span some distance
towards You with dreams made from this hope.
Ah, hope, that strange and elusive flow,
touching our inward man,
causing us to rise up to performance without measure.
The lack of which bringing men to their death,
before their bodies ever cease to function.
A strange thing—this charged up vessel,
filled with dreams and hopes to inspire more.
Have you known such a one?
They leap upon you with vigorous assaults of inspiration,
taking you by the hand into their dreams,
where with hope's light they dazzle you.
A strange thing this walking death is too,
Man, without hope, man without dreams.

Have you seen such a one?

Such longing in their eyes, such pain in their voices.

They too will take you by the hand and lead,

you away from that hope with which you dream your dreams.

I am familiar with both, as are you.

The life abundant which hope supplies,

as radiant dreams.

The despair and death in dreams destroyed,

by hope's departure.

Is this not the perilous thing which man does fear,

more than all else?

That hope will not endure, till dreams are all fulfilled?

More than death itself this is feared, I think.

But, what can death rob me of,

if my hopes and dreams transcend the grave?

If I look beyond to life eternal in You.

There is no thief who can steal such hope.

But what of dreams that stay this side of the grave?

Surely hope's departure can bring them down,

And often will hasten the very hour of death itself.

That is why I say:

Since man is prone to dream his dreams,

Then let my dreams be formed in You.

For you are where no thief can dwell.

I hope in You, and from this hope my dreams are
formed.

I hear You speak, and thus my dreams are born.

I dream of a fullness of life in this Your world,

and of a place beyond to dwell where hope,

can be forgotten.

Where dreams are all fulfilled,

and in glorious splendor surpass the dreamer's visions.

For such a place, I hope and dream.

For such a time, I dream with hope.

Hope, we are told, is an anchor of the soul, both
sure and steadfast, and which enters the Presence behind
the veil (Hebrews 6:19). It is one thing for those in the
world to lose their hope, a hope based in men, but another
for Christians to lose their hope, a hope based upon the
promises of God. These promises guarantee us peace with
God (see Romans 5:1), the assurance of a Helper and of a
Comforter (see John 14:16), as well as the promise of an
abundant life which is our destiny.

The following chapters will be devoted to inspiring
those Christians back to this abundant life that is based
upon the promises of God and is secured by faith in those
promises. It is the love for God that is shed abroad in our

hearts by the Holy Spirit that will compel us to pursue these things. I state them here knowing that faith comes, and I believe can be rekindled, "by hearing and hearing by the Word of God" (Romans 10:17). Faith is a gift of God. Hope and faith, along with love, are the essentials of the Christian life. Without them we cannot please God, for to be without these things is to be without God in the world. God is love and our faith is in Him. "And now abide faith, hope, love, these three; but the greatest of these is love" (1 Corinthians 13:13).

It is my prayer that His love abides in us and draws us away from the distractions of this world so that we may know our inheritance in Christ, and thus walk with assurance in the destiny that He has for us. We are to live *in* this world while not being *of* this world, which means not being devoted to this world. Let us begin with faith in this promise that comes to us from the mouth of the Savior and Lord Jesus Christ Himself, "Ask, and it will be given to you; seek, and you will find; knock, and it will be opened to you. For everyone who asks receives, and he who seeks finds, and to him who knocks it will be opened." (Matthew 7:7-8) In doing these we become Destiny Seekers.

* * *

In *Destiny Seekers* a young man was born into the kingdom of God through a divine experience and began his walk of faith. It is through the use of allegory that we follow his pursuit of the high places formed for God's redeemed. Through all the joys and sorrows, great highs and disappointing lows that we all face in our journey, he found purpose in seeking out the destiny that the Lord had for him. His journey ended half way up the mountain.

In *Two Sides of the Mountain* we take up with this young man again as he continues his pursuit of the high places. Solomon, one of the main characters in this book, might be said to be the culmination of all the wise individuals who have guided him in his walk of faith throughout the years.

I believe that one of the signs of maturity in the faith is when we seek after those things that have eternal value rather than those that have temporal value. That is one of the most difficult challenges that face our generation today. To learn to live in pursuit of the things that have eternal value is what keeps us moving on with God. The things of temporal value are only relevant here in this life, though they can give much joy and comfort, they do not lead us to pursue those things above where Christ is seated at the right hand of the Father.

The things above are higher and we must continue to pursue them, climbing that mountain in pursuit of the place formed for God's redeemed. The climb is the only thing that keeps the church awake and alert.

CHAPTER 1

Memories

"IT'S AMAZING," I THOUGHT, as I sat pondering my life upon the mountain. Looking downward, I realized that I had been climbing this same mountain for over thirty years. When I consider all the camps that I had entered, remaining in some of them for years, I thank the Lord of the mountain that He had urged me on in my pursuit of the higher places. I believe I am nearing the top now. The diary that I kept during my climb was called *Destiny Seekers* because it was at the bottom of this mountain that I began to discover I have a destiny in the Lord. It was on this mountain that I found others with whom I could travel, for they were also seeking their destiny. We were destiny seekers with a heart after the Lord of the mountain. Together we learned the songs from the stream and the words carried on the wind. I have never forgotten the song the Lord gave me to sing as I made my way up the mountain.

Look higher than the mountain,
Don't cast your eyes toward ground,
Seek to pierce the clouds on high,
With gaze towards heaven now be found.
Don't stop at lofty peaks to dwell,
Where man can climb and victory tell,
But long to soar beyond man's means
To places formed for God's redeemed.
Look higher than the mountain,
To where the flowing stream begins,
The source is not in snowcapped peaks,
It has it's start where all things end.

Those "places formed for God's redeemed," yes, that's where I wanted to be when all was said and done. Of all the things I have learned, while climbing the mountain, and all the many experiences I've enjoyed or fled from, one thing has remained a mystery for me. There was that one time, whether in a dream or a vison, I can't remember, when I had veered off the path to go and see what was on the other side of the mountain. I had never been there before. Our path led us straight up the mountain on this one side. I thought about the other side for I'd heard men often speak of it. I remembered finding evidence of the other side in the Bible and that the Lord led me, in a dream or a vision, to a path leading to the other side. For a time, I left my companions and went to see what I might find. What I found on the other side of the mountain was that nation spoken of so often in the Book, the nation of Israel. I could see their flags flying in the various camps they had constructed on their side of the mountain. I could see their structures rising into the sky just like ours did on our side of the mountain. I could also see some of them pursuing the top of the mountain just as many were doing on our side of the mountain. While watching their pursuit, I remembered thinking how it was inevitable that we one day should meet at the top of the mountain. The dream or vision had ended, with the thought of our meeting. Now the thought had returned.

I had separated myself from the others who were climbing with me, just to spend some time thinking about my life. Sitting here on one of the high cliffs, allowing that familiar steady breeze to refresh me, I began to think of Israel. I opened the Bible and began to read of the nation that had come forth from a covenant which the Lord had made with the patriarchs. These patriarchs were certainly the original high climbers. They were the ones who had met the Lord of the mountain face to face. These were the ones whose words we were to listen to. The words were not only their own, but, much of the time, they were the words of the Lord of the mountain given to them as instruction for all who would climb it. Indeed, I thought, these words were given for all the climbers on both sides of the mountain. Then why were we not climbing together, I wondered? I began to realize that the words of the prophets and patriarchs were the very same words that the Lord of the mountain had spoken when He had come to the mountain and walked among us—on the other side of the mountain, not on this side. He had sent His disciples to come to this side of the mountain, and even out to the sea beyond, with the instructions for climbing the mountain. However, while He was here among us, He remained on the other side. I wanted to know more about these men with whom the Lord of the mountain had entrusted both the speaking and recording of these instructional words. I was sure that a greater knowledge of these things would give my pursuit of the high places a fuller meaning. I felt I had gained a great deal of understanding and knowledge through my pursuit up the mountain thus far, but I was sure that there was more. I wanted it. Considering these things, I began to get excited. I felt the kind of excitement returning that had so often filled me in my pursuit up the mountain. After a while I grew weary of the climb because, for a time, I had not heard from the Lord of the mountain. I had not received any new songs from the Great Musician. Things were moving along well with our climb. Most of the time my companions and I were in full agreement, but it was the songs and the dreams that always brought new life into the camp. It had been a long time since we had received a new song or dream. These songs and dreams were never meant to add to the words of the Book. Instead they were meant to give greater revelation concerning our destiny as it related to the instruction found in the Book. The Bible is the book that we referred to almost every day on our journey and so it came to be referred to simply as the Book. Now, however, I felt that I was once again receiving a word from the Lord. It was a word about those on the other side of the mountain. I quickly got to my feet and ran back to my companions who were a short distance from the cliff. I shouted out that all things would become new again. Not new, different things, old things that would become new. Just as when the ancient paths had become new to us, now the old words would become new. They would take on new meaning, a deeper meaning. I was confident, I told them, that revelation was about to spring forth. These words will become life for us! We will be given a new understanding! With that announcement, they too were filled with excitement. We all gathered round, knelt and prayed that it would be so.

CHAPTER 2

The Divine Appointment

OVER THE COURSE OF the next few weeks, I further considered these new things. If I had taken such an interest in the other side of the mountain, could there be someone from the other side of the mountain just as curious about this side? Could there actually be someone from the other side of the mountain here on this side of the mountain? While pondering this my thoughts turned into a prayer, and I began to realize that the Lord of the mountain was birthing within me, not a song, not a dream, but a prayer. He was leading me to pray for a meeting, a divine appointment. I began asking for a meeting with an individual from the other side of the mountain with whom I could converse. I knew that I was full of curiosity about the other side of the mountain, but I wasn't yet sure what my questions were. Thoughts began to flood my mind. Where would the conversation begin? What if we had disagreements right away? Who would resolve the disagreements? Should he ask me a question, would I have the answer? How would we meet? Why should he want to converse with me? Then that familiar voice interrupted this stream of thoughts and simply said, "Trust Me."

People on the mountain would often ask me, "How do you know it's the Lord's voice you're hearing?" I'd tell them that it is not so much a distinct deep voice or anything like that, but rather it is what He is saying that brings to me the knowledge of who is speaking. I have found that every voice in my head wants to lead me to do something, to speak something or to withhold me from something. In my flesh, I often will want to do or speak something that is not life giving or does not advance my destiny of seeking the high places. In my flesh, I often will devise a way of avoiding the pursuit of the high places. When He speaks to me, He is always leading me to speak truth and life. He urges me to continue on in Him, fulfilling my destiny. He seeks to halt my pursuit of fleshly desires. I have learned to trust His voice. Yet, I must learn it over and over again.

I have also learned that He has so created us that He can speak to us through many means. He may speak to us through a dream, perhaps because, when we are asleep, we are not able to brush off His desire to speak to us, as we might do when awake. The issue then becomes whether we will then take the time to examine our dreams and see if He may be trying to communicate something to us.

The Apostle Paul, one of those who was sent to this side of the mountain to teach us, told us that the Lord of the mountain speaks to us through creation. We must, therefore, look at creation with the hope of discovering those things that He would teach us both of Himself and of His creation. When spring fills the air after a long hard winter, we often appreciate the new life that we see unfolding all around us. Is our Lord Jesus speaking something to us in this? Do we need to understand that this new life within creation comes forth in response to Divine command? Does the God of creation command new life for us? Do we need the assurance of new life springing forth after a time of hardship? If indeed we allow Him to speak to us through His creation, we come to understand through the seasons that He is a God of new beginnings. New beginnings bring hope to those who have found ruin in their lives due to events that have carried them into despair.

Then there is that still small voice within, which we so often ignore. If it is the Lord speaking, there is nothing still or small about the voice once we acknowledge that it is He who is speaking. We are told that His Word is living and powerful and sharper than any two-edged sword, piercing even to the division of soul and spirit, and of joints and marrow, and is a discerner of the thoughts and intents of the heart. That doesn't sound still or small to me.

The Lord is faithful to let us know when it is He who is speaking to us by confirming His words to us through conversation with someone else. It becomes a witness to what we may have let pass through our mind without giving acknowledgement and true consideration to what He had previously spoken. When in conversation, someone speaks the very thoughts that had passed through our minds, we are awakened to the possibility that the Lord had spoken to us and is now repeating it through a more obvious means.

Perhaps we will be led to read a passage from the Scriptures which gives us a third witness that He is speaking to us. The Bible tells us that through the witness of two or three, a thing is established. So often, when we read the words recorded in the Bible, the Lord will provide an answer to a life situation. This, too, is Him speaking, if we will recognize His voice. The Spirit and the Word inform and lead us. Through the knowledge and awareness of all these ways in which we hear His voice, our prayer becomes a conversation. We begin by thanking Him that He fills us with His word through dreams, visions, thoughts that drift into our minds, and through conversations with others who know Him. We then acknowledge that we have heard Him and ask Him to explain the dream, the vision, the word.

I had sat considering these things long enough and knew it was time for me to return to those with whom I was traveling. He not only speaks to us, but He also leads us. And it was time to look for His leading in prayer with the others.

The Lord spoke to me and I learned that I needed to pray that He would lead me to one with whom I would enter into a holy conversation. I was not supposed to go in search of this person for that would distract me from my pursuit of the high places—my true destiny. I needed to continue my pursuit while at the same time to be watchful, trusting Him to bring all of it about in His time. I remembered the time I had gotten my first dream from Him. It was three years before I was actually to walk it out with wisdom and understanding. Yet, when it happened, I knew it was the fulfillment of the dream. I must now have confidence in Him that I would know when He would bring about the answer to my prayer.

You see, the Lord knows what we will ask before we ask it. It is not for His sake that we pray, but for our sakes. Prayer keeps us alert to look for the answers to our prayers and also keeps that vital line of communication open between us and the Father. We cannot follow Him if we do not clearly hear and see Him leading us through a prayerful conversation with Him and the events that follow.

CHAPTER 3

The Settlement

SEVERAL MORE MONTHS WENT by while continuing our journey upward. There always came reasons to halt our pursuit. We did this many times. However, we had just begun to start on our way again, when over the next rise appeared a path leading into the woods. Although it would take us off the main trail that we had been traveling, we discussed it and decided to follow the path just to see where it led. It was obvious that some had journeyed this way before for it was well worn. We had only gone a very short distance through the woods when we came upon a vast open valley within the mountain. It was breathtaking. It appeared to stretch from one side of the mountain to the other. A glistening stream ran through it. Near the middle of the valley was a settlement. We reasoned that the path was not too far off the main trail, at least not so far that we couldn't easily find our way back and debated whether or not to visit the settlement and agreed to see what it might have to offer. The valley was so large that it took us several hours to reach the community. Just outside the colony, we passed groves and all kinds of fruit trees. As we approached, people came out to greet us. They seemed genuinely excited to see us and exclaimed how glad they were to see we had progressed so far up the mountain. They invited us in and quickly sent men and women out to gather some of the produce that grew nearby. We were all very excited and began to indulge in their hospitality.

As we sat and conversed with them they told us that their settlement was established by command of the Lord of the mountain. Their responsibility was to greet and encourage those who desired to continue to climb the mountain. I told one of them that it seemed the climb would never end, that the mountain seemed to go on and on. "Does it go on forever?" I asked? Since starting, we had never been able to see the top due to the clouds that constantly surrounded the summit. He simply said, "Yes. It is the climb of a lifetime." What did he mean? Was he saying that it was the biggest event in a lifetime, or that it takes a lifetime to experience the event of reaching the top? We were interrupted so I didn't get to ask. One thing I did know was that it was a mountain of mysteries and the Lord of the mountain seemed pleased to unfold those mysteries for us as we climbed. He did not disclose them all at once, but rather line by line, precept by precept, as the Book states, like the climb itself, one step at a time. They encouraged us to stay for a season, as they put it, inviting us to learn from them some of the things necessary to climb higher.

As we had entered this settlement, I had noticed a log cabin off in the distance. It was so far away that I could hardly see it except for some smoke seemingly rising out of a chimney. Every once in a while, as we went about our daily routine, which included learning more about the history of the mountain, I noticed the little cabin. Finally, my curiosity got the best of me, and I asked one of the men in the camp who it was that lived so far away from the settlement. He said I would need to bring my question to one of the shepherds in the camp. I thought it was a strange reply to my question. With my curiosity piqued, right away I sought out one of their shepherds and asked him why the cabin was so far from the settlement, just sitting out there on its own. He explained it belonged to one of the climbers from the other side of the mountain and that he was separated due to disagreements on how to climb the mountain. Immediately, the word and the prayer that I would meet someone from the other side of the mountain came to mind. I felt a burst of energy inside me. It seemed to be a mixture of excitement at the possibility of fulfilling my prayer and of fear at what the possibility might bring. The shepherd with whom I was conversing cautioned me about seeking this man out. "He has some strange ideas about things," he said. "You'll just end up confused." My hope, however, was that some of my confusion would be cleared up. Even though I knew the Lord of the mountain had taught me a great deal about the Book, there were many things that remained a mystery for me and other things that led to confusion. These things I just had to set aside after reading them, gaining no real understanding or conclusions. I had been able to table them for a time, for years actually, but now I wanted—no needed to know. I felt that what the Lord had me praying about would lead to the answer. I also felt that I could not pass up this opportunity to meet a man from the other side of the mountain. After all, I reasoned, we were pursuing the same thing, the high places formed for God's redeemed. I decided that tomorrow I would leave my traveling companions who had come with me into the settlement and go to this man.

I prayed into the night and sought the Lord to guide me as I had always prayed, "Lord if this is Your will, then give me the courage to walk it out, and if it is not, please stop me." I slept little that night. The next day my flesh was telling me to put it off until another time because I was so very tired. I silenced my flesh and set out for the cabin. I had already explained to the others that I would return to them when the Lord made it clear that I should. I encouraged them to remain in the settlement unless they believed that the Lord was telling them to continue on with their climb. In which case, I would catch up with them at some point.

It took a while to reach the cabin, and as I approached the door an elderly man stepped out onto the porch. He was dressed in rather strange clothing. He had what I would later learn was a prayer shawl over his shoulders with knotted tassels, which I later learned were called Tzitzit, hanging from each side. He also had on his head what I referred to as a beanie, until I was politely told it was called a yarmulke. He opened both of his arms wide and said, "Hello, my name is Solomon, welcome to my home. Come in and rest, and I will get us something to drink. You can then tell me why you have come." I accepted his hospitality and stepped inside to what was to be the most holy conversation that I would ever have.

CHAPTER 4

Getting Settled In

THIS MAN SEEMED TO be one of the most kind and gentle men I had ever met. How could he possibly be a threat to the settlement? You could see the kindness in his eyes. As he continued to listen to me, he brought food to the table. I think he would have offered me all he had to eat in the cabin if I were inclined to keep eating. As he was setting cheese on the table along with some bread, he noticed the Book in my pack. Pointing to the Book, he asked, "Is this what you wish to talk about?" It was as if the Lord had told him I was coming and why I was there. I said, "Yes, it is one of the things that I would like to speak with you about." He then asked, "Are you willing to stay until the conversation is finished?" I told him I would, and he immediately responded by saying, "I will make up the spare room for you then." Noticing my look of surprise as he got up from the table, he said, "Did you think we could discuss this in a few hours? Do not measure the time, measure the progress of the conversation." He then instructed me to make myself at home and walked up a set of stairs.

Still chewing on my bread and cheese, I stood to my feet and began to scout out the cabin. It was simply decorated. I noticed some very interesting things that I had never seen before. Upon entering the front door, the kitchen sat to the right and on the other side of the cabin was a large sitting room containing these unusual things. Setting on a small table up against the wall was a long sheep's horn and beside it a candle holder with seven candles in it as well as various other items placed around the room. I knew, that these items must have some significant meaning and I anticipated talking about these things when the time came. I walked through the sitting room to the back of the cabin where there was what appeared to be a library of sorts. As I entered this room, I could see that this man loved to read. He had a desk in the room and a stand holding a large opened Book. I moved to where I could read the Book but quickly discovered that I couldn't read it. It was written in another language. There were, however, many books written in my language, so I left the large Book and began to pull some of the other books from the book cases. So many books with interesting and exciting titles caught my eye, and I began going from shelf to shelf, from book case to book case, loading up my arms with books. Well, I thought, if I'm going to be here for a while I might as well do some reading. After all, he did tell me to make myself at home.

Solomon entered the room and looked at me with my hands full of books and smiled. "Yes, my friend indulge yourself in these. It will make our conversation much easier and full of meaning. A sharp mind will benefit us both. Come I will show you to your room and you can freshen up and read a little while I prepare our evening meal."

He led me up the stairs and with a gesture of his hand, invited me to enter what would be my room for as long as I was to remain. After I entered the room, he closed the door behind him, and I could hear him going down the stairs. I immediately sat on the freshly made bed and plopped the books down. Taking hold of one with the title of *Zion*, I opened it up and began to read its contents page. Going down through the chapter titles, I could see that it was a book about the history of the Jewish people, and I surmised it would tell me something about their ascent up the mountain. I was so excited that I started reading it and continued until I heard the call for me to join Solomon for our meal. I had not yet told him my name, so he simply called me son. I had been reading for almost an hour and never did freshen up or even move from the bed. I called down that I would be right there and quickly washed my hands and face in the bathroom adjoining my room. As I entered the kitchen, I noticed the candle flickering on the table. He was standing on the other side of the table with his hands on the chair in front of him. With a warm smile on his face he said, "If you would remain standing I would like to welcome in the Sabbath and thank the Creator for His kindness in leading you here and for His provision and to ask also for His blessing upon our very important conversation. Would you agree with that?" I nodded my head in agreement and he began to pray. When he had finished praying, he kindly motioned for me to sit. He pulled out his chair and said, "Now, let's enjoy our meal." After the meal we stayed awhile at the table. He then asked me to excuse him, stating that he had some things to attend to and invited me to relax in the living room or to retire to my room. I chose to go to my room where I continued reading *Zion*.

CHAPTER 5

The Holy Conversation:
It's a Matter of History

THE NEXT MORNING, I was awakened by the smell of food that Solomon was cooking. Was he going to be my teacher or my servant? How could I expect him to supply my needs without some kind of payment? The problem was I didn't have anything to give him. I thought for a moment and then decided that, for as long as I would stay with him, I would offer to do things around the cabin or perhaps run errands for him or do whatever I could to help.

Even though I had stayed up quite late the previous night reading the book, I still felt well rested when I awoke. We had talked for a while after our meal the previous night, before he excused himself. He never initiated a conversation about the Book, so I didn't either. I was sure that he would today. I rose from the bed, got ready for the day, and proceeded down the stairs. He greeted me with a smile. "Did the fragrance of the food wake you?" he asked.

I told him that it smelled wonderful. He said, "Good, it was prepared yesterday. I simply warmed it for us. Let's begin the day by acknowledging the One who blesses. In doing this, we will prepare for our conversation to begin." After praying, he invited me to add a word of gratitude. I gave thanks for the day and its provision. We sat down and enjoyed our meal.

When we had finished he asked, "What is it that you wish to know?" I said that I was aware that there were climbers on both sides of the mountain and I wondered, if we were all pursuing the same thing, which is to reach the top of the mountain, then why did we not climb together, assisting one another? He said, "It is good that you wish to know this."

I interrupted and said, "I want to know if the Book tells me the answer to my question."

He said, "Yes, indeed, the Book, but first we must begin with the history of the side of the mountain with which you are not familiar. Only then can you understand what you seek in the Book. It is absolutely necessary that you understand the history in order to understand the word of God at the deeper level." I asked him about the large book on the stand in his study. He said, "Yes, that is called the Tanakh. It is written in Hebrew, the original language from which your Book was translated. It is necessary to go back to the original language and to understand the meaning of words in that language to truly understand what the Creator wants us to know of

Him and of His creation." I asked him how someone who didn't know the Hebrew language could do that. He told me that many ways have been provided for those who wish to know. He said, "You call your book the Bible. It is a collection of books including the Jewish writings that we call the Tanakh. You say that it is the word of God and so it is. For the most part, the people on my side of the mountain do not accept what you call the New Testament as the inspired word of God, but you do. However, some of us do accept that it is the inspired word of God and that it offers much that can lead to a greater understanding of our Tanakh."

I then asked, "Are you saying that you believe the Jesus of the New Testament is the Messiah?"

"Yes, I am saying that, however I do not know Him, blessed be His name, as Jesus. He was a Hebrew with a Hebrew name. His name is Yeshua, which in Hebrew means salvation. It is because of this belief that I was sent here to await the arrival of those who come, as you have, to understand the Hebraic roots of your faith. Are you aware that this is what you are seeking? You see, though there are two sides of the mountain, it is one mountain." He then took a sip of his tea, all the time looking at me straight in the eyes. I sat there pondering what I had just heard. Once again, I thought to myself, what is so threatening about this man?

"I noticed that you were up late last night," he said. "I could see the light coming from your room under the door. Were you reading from one of the books that you brought to your room from my study?"

"Yes", I replied, "I began reading from the book titled *Zion*."

"Ah yes, that is good," he said, "It will help in our conversation about the history of my side of the mountain. Do you know what the word *Zion* means or what Zion is?"

"To some extent", I replied.

"Well then let's begin there."

"The meaning of the word *Zion* is 'protect, defend, hence a place of defense'. However, it has a much broader meaning than that. Zion is mentioned over 150 times in the TaNaKh. It is the prophet Samuel who first speaks of it. He tells us that David captured this place from the Jebusites and that it became known thereafter as the City of David. Surely you have read of David, king of Israel, in your Bible."

"Oh yes, he is one of my favorite people in the Bible," I replied. "I love to sing his psalms. We all do—those with whom I travel."

"And where are those with whom you travel?"

"I believe that they are still at the settlement, in the valley."

"Yes, I know where it is" he said. And why did they not come with you here to my house?" "The shepherds of the settlement were uneasy about my coming here, so I told the others to wait for me there or to go on with their climb and I would catch up with them," I answered.

"Yes, unfortunately it is very hard to hear something that seems contrary to what you have accepted as the truth all of your life," he responded. "I have tried to have a conversation with some of the shepherds in the settlement, but there are many things to get past before we can have an open conversation. "I understand this well. I was in a similar place and could not accept that Yeshua is the Messiah of Israel until I was able to see outside of the traditions of my people. I could not see beyond what I had been taught and believed to be the truth all my life until the scales fell from my eyes, just as they did from the eyes of Saul, the apostle you call Paul. Traditions are often meant to fortify a truth, but sometimes they can replace the truth. Now, you are here. If we are able, by the grace of the Lord of this mountain, to enter into and finish this holy conversation, then perhaps we can both be used by our Lord to speak to those who will listen on both sides of the mountain. Now, back to *Zion*."

"May I ask a question first?" I said.

"Of course," he responded.

"When you say that it is important to understand history in order to understand the words of God through the prophets, you mean the history recorded in the Bible, right?"

"I did not say that it was important, I said that it was absolutely necessary. You see, biblical history, in and of itself, is prophetic. This is one of the biblical principles that you must learn. It is also necessary to learn the importance of words such as *Zion.* The biblical use of this one word allows us to see a literal place, a people, a reference to Messiah, and the plan of the God of Israel to rescue His people. Mount Zion is synonymous with the temple and with Jerusalem. There are times when it includes the entire nation of Israel, the covenant people of God. It stands for the city of God in the coming age. Yahweh identifies Himself as the One who dwells on Mount Zion. This is where He begins His work of salvation, and this is where He will judge mankind. There are many things that we shall touch upon using Zion as a stepping stone into these things."

"Can you give me a few examples of what kind of things you are referring to," I asked?

"Yes, I will give you some things to consider as you read your Bible and then we will have a deeper discussion of them as we move along with our conversation. Psalm 48 tells us that Zion is the 'joy of the whole earth.' Look at this Psalm and consider why Zion is the joy of the whole earth. I believe that the book *Zion* will inform you that Zion is the place where Adonai's great deeds of salvation will take place during the earthly reign of Yeshua. Oh, the list goes on and on. The prophet Isaiah tells us that the God of Israel will build the city by laying a precious cornerstone in Zion. He further tells us that the God of Israel will protect the inhabitants of Zion in the coming great day of the Lord, in much the same way He protected the children of Israel in Egypt during the Exodus. The prophet declares that God's people will return in joy and gladness to Zion from the nations of the world to which they have been scattered. This is the great hope of those on my side of the mountain. This is why the people climb. It is in expectation of the gathering of the people and the restoration of the whole house of Israel. We will discuss this further in the days ahead. It, too, will become a part of our conversation. Both the prophet Isaiah and Micah tell us that people will come from every nation of the earth to worship here at Mount Zion. Both Isaiah and Zechariah tell us that Yeshua Himself will reign from Mount Zion for a thousand years and then into eternity. My son, you have much to consider. Go and read your book, but before we part, let us give thanks to Him who gives knowledge to the simple and makes wise the humble."

I was beginning to see the Christlike character in this man. My question had been answered. He was certainly the teacher, as well as one who was not here to be served, but to serve. He is not leader *or* servant, but both. I remembered the particular passage in the Bible where Jesus, now Yeshua throughout the rest of our conversation, said that he who wanted to be the greatest in the kingdom of God must become the servant of all. Solomon was here both to teach and to serve those whom the Lord of the mountain would send to him. He had received and learned the truths given by the Lord of the mountain to those on both sides of the mountain. He had set aside the traditions which masked as God's truth and then had gained an understanding of the Word of God and embraced the truths given in the whole Bible. In so doing Solomon had come to understand that Yeshua is the Messiah. The whole Bible was opened to him, and he understood it to be one book. It was no longer the new versus the old or one part excluding the other. For it is the whole counsel of the God of Israel, all relevant today and important in the ascent to the top of the mountain, to those places formed for God's redeemed. I now knew that this was indeed the answer to my prayer. I was eager to learn from this man, and, if the Lord was willing, I could offer something from the knowledge I had gained through my climb on my side of the mountain. It would truly be a conversation, a holy conversation. After he prayed he returned to his Book on the stand and I to my room.

Solomon did indeed give me much to consider. As I sat in the chair in my room looking out the window, I began to think about Zion. Rather than read *Zion* at that moment, I wanted to consider all that we had just talked about downstairs. I started to think about what he said concerning tradition replacing truth. I didn't know much about the traditions on his side of the mountain, so I began to think about those on my side of the mountain. Then I remembered he had asked me if I came in search of the Hebraic roots of my faith. I looked out the window and at the clouds that hid the top of the mountain. Were our traditions hiding the very truths of God so that we could not see clearly what the truth of God really is? Were these truths to be found by returning to the Hebraic roots of Christianity?

In my mind, I began to sort the traditions out from the biblical truths that I thought were evident and supported the traditions. Then I realized what I was doing. I was looking for the biblical support for traditions rather than the support that traditions were supposed to give to biblical truth. I realized then and there that this reverse thinking is what I had been trained to do within the camps upon my side of the mountain. The more amens that were given to these traditions by the people, the more sound and valid they seemed to be. But did God say amen to them? Doctrines were formed around these traditions. Men searched Scripture to support the doctrines. It seemed to be backward. I then heard His voice saying to me, "Be as the Bereans." I remembered that the Bereans were those mentioned in the Bible who searched the Scriptures daily to find out whether the things being spoken by the apostle were true. Did his words line up with the words of Moses and the prophets? I knew I could not keep these things straight in my mind, so I searched the desk drawer to see if I could find paper and pen. There they were in the middle drawer almost as if Solomon knew I would have need of them. I quickly made two columns on the piece of paper and began to write down all the traditions I could think of that were held to on my side of the mountain. The next task would be to see if they celebrated and supported biblical truth. I prayed that the Lord would guide me in this effort. I determined that I would lead the conversation from my notes the next time Solomon and I got together. I also made this note: In search of the Hebraic roots of my faith.

CHAPTER 6

The Holy Conversation: What about Tradition

SOLOMON NEVER NEEDED TO call me for a meal unless I was outside. The fragrance of whatever he was cooking would rise right up the stairs and into my room. I knew it was time for the evening meal, so I washed up, went downstairs, and watched Solomon at the stove singing a song to the Lord of the mountain. Before entering the kitchen, I stood there at the bottom of the stairs and listened to his song. He had a deep voice with a slight accent. His singing right then made me feel more at home than I had up to that point. The words he sang were in Hebrew: *Shalom bimromav he ya' ase shalom alenu v'al kol Y'ISRAEL V'imroo, v'imroo Amein.* I would later learn the words to the song in my own language: 'May He who makes peace from high above make sweet shalom, for all of us, and for all Israel and say, and say, Amen!' It didn't matter that I didn't know what he was singing at the time, it was comforting just to listen to him. He stopped singing and said, "Come into the kitchen, my son, you can't partake from the hallway." I grinned and entered the kitchen. He had known I was there the whole time. He turned away from the stove to face me and asked, "Do you like to sing?"

"Yes, I do. I especially like to sing unto the Lord. I like to sing about His love and His grace and mercy."

"Good! We will sing together. I will teach you songs and you shall teach me songs. This will be the first thing in which we shall unite from both sides of the mountain. With songs of praise to our God. We shall sing the songs of Zion."

Ah, there was that word again, *Zion*. "Will we continue our conversation after our meal?" I asked. "I would like to talk about tradition, if we could."

"Yes, let's talk about tradition," he responded. We gave thanks for the meal we were about to eat and added a request for blessing upon our conversation that evening. After we finished I cleared the table and washed the dishes, trying to offer what I could by way of payment for his charity. I also told him as long as I was there, I would take care of bringing in the wood for the stove as well as, chopping and stacking it.

I eagerly ran up the stairs, went into my room, collecting my Bible, the book on Zion, and my notes. When I entered the sitting room expecting Solomon to be waiting for me, I found he wasn't there. I stood in the dimly lit room listening for him. His voice was coming from his study. The door was partially opened, so I walked across the parlor and peaked my head in. Solomon was standing in front of the large Book and was reading aloud. He first would read from the Tanakh in the Hebrew language, and then he would pray in English. I felt I was intruding on something personal and private. As I began stepping back, I heard him say, "Come in and join me in prayer."

"I don't want to intrude," I responded.

"You are not intruding if I invite you in. Come and sit there. First, I will read and then I will tell you what I have read and then we can pray together. Does that seem good to you?"

"Yes."

He then shared with me that he was reading from the prophet Isaiah about the Gentiles blessing Zion. What a surprise, I thought to myself. It has to do with Zion. It was then that I realized that I was not going to control the conversation and that we most likely were not going to talk about tradition. He read the verse in Hebrew from the TaNaKh, he closed his eyes, and spoke the entire verse in English from memory. "Arise, shine; for your light has come! And the glory of the LORD is risen upon you. For behold, the darkness shall cover the earth, and deep darkness the people; but the LORD will arise over you, and His glory will be seen upon you. The Gentiles shall come to your light, and kings to the brightness of your rising."

Then he began to pray. He prayed for the fulfillment of this prophetic word given to Isaiah (60:1-3). He asked if I understood the passage. I said that I thought I did, "But why did you pray for its fulfillment? Wasn't it fulfilled with the coming of Yeshua?"

"No" he said. "This is one of the great issues that divide the climbers on both sides of the mountain. You see, those on my side of the mountain await the fulfillment of those very things which are taught to have already been fulfilled on your side of the mountain. The TaNaKh and your Bible both tell us that unless two are agreed, they cannot walk together. There are many things we are not agreed upon concerning the great prophetic Scriptures. That which I have just prayed for is to take place in the future. It has to do with the covenant promise of the God of Israel to regather the exiles of Israel who were scattered into the nations of the world. Some call this the Greater Exodus at the end of the age. Within this whole chapter, Isaiah is speaking of the glory of Jerusalem and Israel in what is called the millennial kingdom, when Messiah rules the whole earth from Jerusalem. We will discuss this further at another time. You said you wanted to discuss tradition, and I said we would. It is very much through the traditions on both sides of the mountain that these truths have been confused and often misplaced within time. You see Yeshua came for the very purpose of uniting the two houses of Israel."

"What do you mean by the two houses of Israel?" I asked.

"Well, after the death of King Solomon, the nation of Israel was divided into two kingdoms, the Northern Kingdom known as Israel and the Southern Kingdom known as Judah. The judgment of God fell upon the Northern Kingdom because of their disobedience. Its people were conquered by the Assyrians and then exiled into the nations of the world. They became assimilated into these nations and lost their identity as the people of God. They no longer held to the Torah, the instruction of God which separated them from other nations. They took on the traditions and ways of those within the kingdoms to which they were scattered. If to England, they became Englishmen, if to France, they became Frenchmen.

The Southern Kingdom, who we call Jews, because Judah was the largest tribe, maintained their identity, even though they were later conquered by the Babylonians. Yeshua said that He was sent for the lost sheep of the house of Israel, the Northern Kingdom. This was His great mission in coming to the earth. He sent His disciples out as fishers of men in order to fulfill what He prophesied through the great prophet Jeremiah who said the Lord spoke to him saying He would send many fishermen to fish out the exiles of Israel from among the nations where they had been scattered."

"But He came so that we might have forgiveness of sins." I rebutted. "He did not come just for those on your side of the mountain. He came to offer the gospel of salvation to the people of the whole world. That is why the camps on my side of the mountain speak so much of the Great Commission, to preach the gospel of salvation to the whole world. That is what brings men from the sea to the mountain."

His response set me back in my chair. "Yes," he said. "There is truth in what you say, but it is not the whole truth. The Great Commission is not simply to preach the gospel of salvation. The Great Commission is also to make disciples and to teach *all* that Yeshua said and did. You see there is the gospel of salvation which is to be preached, however, the gospel of salvation is only a part of the gospel of the kingdom. The people on your side of the mountain do not understand the gospel of the kingdom that the people on my side of the mountain embrace and lift in prayer. They understand what the prophets foretold would take place *within* the kingdom of Israel. They do not accept the gospel of salvation in its place. It is the gospel of salvation that the people on your side of the mountain embrace, but they do not understand that it is only a part of the gospel of the kingdom. Therefore, they do not understand what we embrace as truth. I will give you something to consider tonight, and then we shall end our conversation for now. It is because of the traditions on my side of the mountain that we were not able to receive Yeshua as the Messiah when He came the first time. We thought that He was trying to destroy our traditions. We thought rightly. He was challenging every tradition within the Judaism of His day that did not support the Torah of Moses and the Prophets. Likewise, it is through traditions that were quickly developed and embraced within Christianity that kept you from truly understanding why Yeshua came. They are still keeping you from understanding the gospel of the kingdom. Thus, each side of the mountain remains separated in our worship of the same God. Yeshua died on the tree to make a way for the forgiveness of sin. Only after sin is forgiven can one embrace the gospel of the kingdom. Therefore, the gospel of salvation must first be preached, and then the gospel of the kingdom is opened to the redeemed, who have received the gospel of salvation. Each side of the mountain holds to a truth, but the traditions of each side remain a stumbling block and create a boundary for both sides. Whenever they do come together, each presenting and accepting the truth that the other holds, then we can enter into that place formed for God's redeemed."

"Wow! That is a great deal to think about," I said. "Both sides of the mountain have valued tradition at the cost of truth and unity."

"Yes, and when one understands this and begins with an open heart to search for the truth, and to separate out all tradition that does not support the truth, then we will be united not by tradition but by truth." he interjected.

I stood to my feet and said, "And the truth shall make you free. Good night, Solomon, I will consider all that you have said tonight. I ask that you pray that the Lord will give me understanding."

"Good night my son," he said.

CHAPTER 7

The Gospel of Salvation

THE GOSPEL OF SALVATION: "For God so loved the world that He gave His only begotten Son that whosoever believes in Him should not perish, but have everlasting life" (John 3:16). While laying on my bed and thinking of our conversation, that passage immediately came to mind. The gospel of salvation is about redemption, but I had never thought of there being two gospels. Wait, there couldn't be two gospels. I remember the Apostle Paul warning the Galatians that if anyone preached any other gospel that they should be accursed. That's pretty strong language. Then there couldn't be two gospels!

I jumped out of bed turned on the light and grabbed my Bible. I went to the concordance in the back and looked up the word *gospel*. Over and over again I found reference to the gospel of the kingdom. Why had I not seen this distinction before? We have always talked about the gospel of salvation. We had also talked about the kingdom of

God and the kingdom of heaven, but the term *gospel* was always discussed as the gospel of salvation. I needed to understand more about this new truth.

After putting my Bible back on the bedside table and turning off the light, I tried in vain to sleep. I could not shut my mind off. I kept thinking and praying for understanding. The last thought I remembered running through my mind was recalling the gospel of salvation as being a part of the gospel of the kingdom and therefore the two are really the same gospel. There is only one gospel. First, the gospel of salvation is preached to the lost. Then the gospel of the kingdom is taught to the redeemed in order to teach and train them to become disciples of Yeshua, ambassadors for Christ. Yeshua did this very thing, teaching His disciples that He was the Savior of Israel. After His resurrection and before His ascension He discipled them and charged them to do the same until He should come again. This was the gospel that Paul preached and taught.

The next morning, I was not awakened by the smell of cooking food but by the sound of Solomon outback chopping wood. Oh no, I thought, I told him that I would take care of the wood supply as long as I was with him. I quickly got dressed and rushed outside to find him swinging an ax.

I said, "Solomon, I'd like to take care of chopping the wood for as long as I am here. I will chop it and stack it and bring it inside as we need it."

He said, "That is very nice of you, but to stop doing it and then have to return to it once you leave will be difficult for me. I must keep on with it in order to maintain my strength." I began to object, and he interrupted me. "My son, we will do it together. That way I will stay physically fit, and you will be of great help to me as well. There is another ax in the shed. Go and get it and we will see if we can split this pile of wood and make room for the next."

I went off to find the ax in the shed. After finding the ax I returned and began splitting wood with Solomon. I had only split a few pieces in the time it took Solomon to split at least a dozen. I couldn't for the life of me figure out what was going on. I was sweating so badly I could hardly see from the sweat running from my forehead into my eyes. I stopped and stood up straight. Solomon began to laugh. I looked at him and he laughed all the more.

"What are you laughing about?" I asked.

"To try and understand the Word of God without prayer and an understanding of the history and culture of the people through whom it came is like chopping wood with a dull ax. It will produce a great deal of sweat but very little productivity."

"You mean you knew the ax was dull?" I complained.

"Of course, that is why it was in the shed. It needs to be sharpened just like your mind," he responded.

"That's funny Solomon," I said. "Where do I go to sharpen it?"

"Your mind or the ax?" he asked through his laughter. Solomon took the ax and gave me the one he was using and then walked toward the shed.

I started to think about the gospel of the kingdom again. When he returned, I asked, "How could the people on your side of the mountain receive the gospel of the kingdom if they hadn't received the gospel of salvation? I thought you said that the gospel of the kingdom must be preached to those who have already received the gospel of salvation otherwise they could not understand it. You said that spiritual things are spiritually appraised, and one must be spiritual to understand them, or something like that."

"Yes, my son, you remembered well," he said. It is because the statutes and ordinances, the very oracles of God were committed to Israel. Israel has the Torah, the commandments, the covenants, and the feasts. Therefore Israel, being a chosen people and God's own possession, has understood spiritual things pertaining to the kingdom of God for generations through the teachings of Moses and the Prophets. However, because their traditions became interwoven with the Torah, they could not recognize a Messiah who would not hold to those traditions and would speak out against them. The same holds true with Christianity today. Those, who now come preaching the gospel of the kingdom as Yeshua taught it from the Torah, appear to be standing against other traditions which have over time been interwoven within Christianity. The fact is that the gospel of the kingdom must and will oppose those traditions that do not celebrate the truth found only in the Holy Scriptures."

He then turned back to the wood pile and grabbed another piece of wood. Handing it to me he stated, "There will be time for more discussion later. Now, you must finish splitting the wood while I go to prepare our breakfast."

I continued splitting the wood with the sharpened ax. My mind was so taken up with the things that Solomon had just shared that it was as if my body was splitting the wood without my mind engaging in it. I soon found that within an hour, I had split all the wood in the pile. I was just about to begin stacking what I had split, when I heard Solomon call me in for breakfast. I went in, washed up, and joined him at the table.

While setting some things on the table, Solomon said, "Let's have a quiet meal. Then I shall go to my study and you to your room to spend some time in prayer." I agreed.

CHAPTER 8

Back to the Stream

ONCE AGAIN, I WAS sitting in my chair by the window looking out over the valley, and I could see a stream off in the distance. The stream brought back memories of my journey up the mountain and all the time I would sit by the stream singing the songs that the Lord of the mountain would bring to me. Picking up my Bible, I went downstairs and knocked on Solomon's study door. I opened the door and told him that I was going for a walk and would be praying as I walked. He didn't turn to look at me but just nodded from under the prayer shawl that was pulled up over his head.

I set out walking down to the stream with the hope of having one of those special visitations by the Holy Spirit. It only took me about ten minutes or so to reach the stream. I looked around for a comfortable spot to sit down to begin my conversation with the Lord of the mountain. There was an old oak tree that looked like it would offer some comfort. Sitting down in its welcoming shade I leaned up against it. Immediately I felt settled. I began by thanking the Lord for His creation and the beauty of it all. I started to take in the sound of the stream as it flowed past me, and to allow the breeze to cool me as it gently swept by. I closed my eyes and thought about my life upon the mountain, reviewing all the major events during my climb. I thought about my companions I had left at the settlement and wondered how they were doing. Were they still at the settlement or had the Lord directed them to move on? I prayed for them.

I began to converse with the Lord asking Him why I was led to Solomon. I believed our conversations were amazing in that I had never before considered many of the things we were discussing. I asked the Lord where it all would lead. What is its purpose? Even if the two of us came to agreement concerning the way one was to climb to the high places, even if we agreed upon everything, what would that accomplish? It would still be just the two of us sitting between the two sides of the mountain. What is next? Where, could it possibly lead?

Then I heard the Lord say, "I have kept for Myself a remnant." I thought about that for a moment, then I heard Him say, "Despise not small beginnings." I had learned that with just a few words, the Lord could communicate things which could take a lifetime to understand and to walk out. "Despise not small beginnings" told me that there was much more than I could possibly imagine ahead of me. Perhaps it was things involving the kingdom. No, not perhaps. I knew it would be things involving the kingdom of God. Why else was He using Solomon to teach me the gospel of the kingdom?

I was distracted by movement out of the corner of my eye. A little way down stream was a deer quietly drinking from the stream. It lifted its head and sniffed the air and then lowered its head. It drank again before lifting its head once more to turn and look behind it. I then saw two fawns come out of a patch of trees. I thought, this must be the mother venturing out ahead of her offspring to make sure it was safe for them to come out and drink from the stream. All three were now safely drinking from the stream. When they had finished, they returned to a cluster of trees and disappeared from my sight. At the moment, I saw no lesson in this for me; however, I had always learned to look for the Lord to speak to me through whatever circumstance He might choose.

Seeing the deer caused me to start thinking of family, which led me further to think of the family of God, which in turn led me right back to the kingdom of God. We were all to be a family within the kingdom of God. I remembered that the scriptures talked about us being sons and daughters of the living God. That makes us a family. Then I thought about what Solomon had previously asked me, about whether I was aware that I was seeking the roots of my faith? Families have roots, heritage. Seeking our roots is seeking our heritage. Since we are brought in and given new life through Yeshua, His heritage is our heritage. He is called our brother as well as our Lord and Savior. He is the firstborn of many brethren. We all have the same heavenly Father. Another piece to the puzzle. It all started making sense to me. I jumped to my feet and said, "Thank you Lord. I'm so glad we had this conversation. I'm going to tell Solomon what you have just shared with me." I headed back to the cabin and found Solomon sitting on the front porch in his rocking chair. "Solomon! I shouted, I want to tell you what the Lord revealed to me in prayer. It's not anything that I didn't already know, but I really didn't realize the fuller meaning until just now."

"Wonderful!" he said. "I have some friends bringing me supplies from my side of the mountain, and they will be here any moment now. They come every week on this day around this time. Can you wait until this evening so that we will not be interrupted in our conversation? I must greet them when they arrive and offer them some refreshment."

"Of course," I said.

"Sit with me here on the porch and enjoy the sunshine. I'd like to introduce you to them when they arrive. It occurs to me that you have been here for several days, and I do not even know your name. I have been calling you son, but I cannot introduce you as son. What is your name?"

"My name is James," I told him.

"Ah James, from the name Jacob. It is a good name, and it suits you for the task He has given you. Do you know that the name Jacob means "supplanter"? While we wait for my friends we can discuss the meaning of your name. Your name means to take by the heel, just as Jacob did to his brother Esau. You must have read the account. Jacob supplanted his brother twice. Do you know what it means to supplant? It means to supersede and replace. Is that what our Lord intends for you, to supersede and replace something? Perhaps maybe the non-biblical traditions on your side of the mountain? That is more to ponder, James."

That was a frightening thought. Despise not small beginnings, indeed.

"It is the Elijah task of our day, James," he said with an almost stern look on his face. "The Elijah task of our day is something dear to my heart, and we will discuss it soon."

Just then the two men Solomon was expecting came into view. As they approached we both stood to our feet and walked down the steps and off the porch to greet them. Solomon hugged each of them and then turned to me and said, "This is James. He is my guest." After greeting each other, I went into the house and up to my room while they visited for the rest of the afternoon.

When the sun started to set I could hear Solomon sending his friends off. Within minutes, I heard the pots and pans being placed on the stove. I wanted to go down and start a conversation, but I learned by now that he did not like to converse while he was preparing a meal. He liked to sing and pray. So, I waited for him to call to me.

CHAPTER 9

The Gospel of the Kingdom

THAT EVENING, AFTER I had finished the dishes and put everything away I headed for Solomon's study expecting to find him at the great Book and praying. Instead I found him at his desk with several books and maps spread out.

I walked over to him and asked, "Are you too busy for our talk this evening?"

He replied, "No, not at all. This is all for you to see as we talk. You have been asking about the gospel of the kingdom. The gospel of the kingdom starts long before Yeshua came to earth. Remember, I told you how essential a knowledge of history is to an understanding of why Yeshua came to earth?"

"Yes, I remember," I responded.

"Well, let's take a journey back tonight, shall we?"

"Sure," I said. What else was I going to say? He had set all this up and prepared for this walk back in time, so I had to say yes. I guess he had forgotten that I was very excited about what I felt the Lord had shown me by the stream. It could wait though. It had made too big an impression on me to ever forget it. He pointed to a chair on the other side of the room. "There," he said. "Bring that chair over here and sit beside me at the desk. Now, before we look at these things, what was it you believe the Lord showed to you at the stream today?"

"Oh, it was aaah, it had to do with family. It might take a long time to discuss what I came to understand, perhaps more time than you want to take tonight after getting all these things laid out."

"Well, on the other hand, it may fit right into this conversation about history," he said. "You see, what I want to discuss with you is all about family. It begins with the family of Abram who is later named Abraham. We can work this in one of two ways. Either you can begin to share with me what you heard today, and I will interject what I think is pertinent from the history of this family, or I can begin to share with you about the history of this family and you can interject what you think is pertinent from what you heard today. Does that seem good to you?"

"Yes, that sounds fine," I said.

"Then which shall it be?"

"Why don't you begin, and I will interject," I said.

"All right then, let's begin."

"You know that Abraham is called our father, don't you?"

"Yes, I know that he is called Father Abraham. I know that the God of Israel made a covenant with him and said that he would be the father of many nations. I also know that the religious rulers of Yeshua's day said that he was their father."

"Yes, that is correct," he said. "Let's focus on the first thing you mentioned. He was called by the God of Israel to be the father of many nations. Now, since this is a covenant promise, made to Abraham, it must come about through the terms or conditions of a covenant. Do you understand what I am saying?"

"I'm not sure because we don't speak much about covenants on my side of the mountain except for the new covenant, or what we call the New Testament," I said.

"Yes, and herein lies one of the major issues between the two sides of the mountain. We do not understand each other's language when it comes to covenant. Let me walk you through the way we understand the Bible to teach covenant. Remember that I told you that words are important, and that, at times, it is necessary to go back to the original language to truly understand what is being communicated?"

"Yes, I remember."

"Well, let's look at the language of what is being communicated in the covenant with Abraham. Here, look on with me as I read from Genesis 17:7. It says, 'And I will establish My covenant between Me and you and your descendants after you in their generations, for an everlasting covenant, to be God to you and your descendants after you' Now, who is establishing this covenant?" he asked.

"God is." I replied.

"Yes, the God of Israel, blessed be His name. He says this is My covenant. So, it is God's covenant and it is made with Abraham and his descendants. Now, when we speak of descendants, we are speaking of family are we not?"

"Yes, that is what the Lord was showing me at the stream today. Family, as it is related to the kingdom. We are supposed to be a family and that is what the gospel of the kingdom is about."

"Yes, my son, that is good. God is good and pleased to teach those who will seek knowledge. It pleases me that He has shown this to you, especially in light of our present conversation. Now, as to the *how* of becoming a family and identifying with the family, this also is explained within the history and heritage of the family according to covenant. It is God's covenant made with Abraham and his descendants. We are further told that it is an everlasting covenant. This is perhaps the most important point concerning covenants. All of God's covenants with man are everlasting covenants. All other covenants that follow this first covenant will simply add to, or further define, this covenant because of its everlasting nature. Most seekers on your side of the mountain believe that the God of Israel made a new covenant with mankind having nothing to do with this Abrahamic covenant. They believe the "old covenant" has been done away with or nailed to the cross as some put it. This, however, cannot be true if one knows the meaning of covenant. It is another one of the things that separates the two sides of the mountain.

Now, since this is a family matter, who are Abraham's descendants? We know that Abraham had two sons named Ishmael and Isaac. So, are all of Ishmael's descendants involved in this covenant? The answer is no. Does that make God a liar? May it never be. It was only those descendants of Abraham defined by the covenant to whom God was speaking. The covenant specifically stated that Abraham would have a son of promise with Sarah, his wife. Ishmael was not the son of promise with his wife Sarah and was, therefore, not included in this covenant. Isaac was that miracle son given to Abraham and Sarah, a descendant according to the covenant. The family had begun.

Isaac was then married to Rebekah and she bore him two sons: Jacob and Esau. Esau sold his birthright. The descendants of Abraham and Isaac would continue on through Jacob and, therefore, the covenant promises would continue only through Jacob and his sons. Jacob had twelve sons who we now know became the twelve tribes of Israel, because God changed Jacob's name to Israel. Now, that family had greatly multiplied, and all the covenant promises are to them and their descendants after them. As long as they put their faith and trust in the God of Israel by obeying the covenant, they would know the blessings associated with the covenant promises. When they turned away from the covenant God of Israel, they would know curses. This is contained in the covenant language, or what may be called the laws of the covenant."

It was time for me to interject. "This whole family thing makes it so much more personal. Even though, at this point, we are talking about twelve tribes, a whole nation, it is each person within each family, within each tribe, within the whole nation, that really matters. These people on your side of the mountain share something that I don't think any other nation has. It is evident that God loved Abraham and because of that love, blessed him. But doesn't He love all the people within every nation of the world as well?"

"Of course, He does, James. This is where the gospel of the kingdom comes in. My son, there is a great deal here to discuss. Let's look at what God promised Abraham and his descendants a little more closely. Open your Bible to Genesis. Take this pen and underline the verses that I will read so that you may make quick reference to them during future conversations. Look here, I have these things underlined in these books. This particular book is all about the covenant with Abraham, and it speaks of each verse that I will have you underline. Take notes as well, so that you can pray for greater understanding. You know our heavenly Father loves for us to pray in this way. On my side of the mountain we believe that one of the greatest forms of worship is the study of His Word.

I will show you some things that are promised in this covenant with Abraham, Isaac, and Jacob, and all Israel.

First, He said that Abraham would become a great nation. Indeed, he has become a great nation. During the reign of his descendants David and Solomon, Israel became the greatest nation on the face of the earth. When Yeshua returns, He will sit on the throne of David ruling over the whole earth and this promise will see its future fulfillment. Thus, this covenant has not yet ended. Next, there is the promised land. We know that the Scriptures speak to us of the promised land. This physical land has been gained and lost through the years, but one day Israel shall possess it for eternity. Always remember the promises of God are true. When He said that Abraham would be greatly blessed, that included all his descendants. He said that his name would be great. Who does not know of Abraham? Who does not know of Israel? God said that Abraham would be a blessing to other nations. One of the ways that he is a blessing to others is through his descendants. For it is written that he who blesses Israel will be blessed. Have you marked all of these things in your Bible?"

"Yes, I did. These are the things we should all want for our families," I said. "God's blessing, land to live on, to have a good name, to be a blessing to our neighbors."

"Yes," he quickly added. "And when these things are not upon and within the family, when the family is separated from them, then something must be done to bring them back. Once again this is where the gospel of the kingdom comes in. There came a time when Israel turned away from their covenant God of Israel. God had to judge them according to the law of the covenant. He also had to remain true to the covenant with Abraham, which is everlasting. So, He promised that He would restore the family, the kingdom, and bring them back from the lands into which they had been dispersed, as a punishment for breaking the covenant. God would bring them back to the promised land and reunite them. Abraham's descendants, the family of Jacob called Israel, would be restored and dwell in the land once again. This is why Yeshua came. As it is written, "He was sent to the lost sheep of the house of Israel" (Matthew 15:24).

"But, He came to offer salvation to everyone who believes in Him and not just to Israel, right," I asked?

"Ah, but this is where we begin to see the amazing wisdom of our God, James. He uses the very punishment for breaking the covenant, that is, the scattering of Israel into the nations where they lose their identity and take on the identity of those nations to which they were scattered, to redeem them. By coming and dying on the tree for the forgiveness of sin, He then sent out the disciples to all the nations of the world preaching the gospel of salvation, and thus bringing them back into the family of Abraham. Remember that one of the blessings given to Abraham and his descendants, unto every generation, was that all nations would be blessed in him or in his descendants?"

"Yes, I'm beginning to see the bigger picture," I said.

He continued, "This too, is part of the gospel of the kingdom, James. Yeshua is descended from Abraham and is of the tribe of Judah. He is called the Lion of the tribe of Judah. He had to first provide the way for the forgiveness of the sins of His people, His family. He had to pay the penalty for their sins and thus satisfy the justice of God, in order to then free the exiles of Israel and unite the family of God. What your side of the mountain calls the new covenant, or the New Testament is actually a renewal of the covenant with Abraham. A covenant being everlasting is never done away with or finished; it is therefore renewed and remains everlasting. This renewed covenant was made with Israel as were all the other covenants from Abraham up to, and including, this final renewed covenant.

Did you know that Abraham is mentioned about one hundred times in the New Testament?" he asked.

"So, if Yeshua came to fulfill the covenant promises made to Abraham and his descendants, then what about the rest of us who aren't Abrahams descendants?" I asked.

"That, James, is what I want you to understand. The Apostle Paul addresses this in his letter to the church at Rome and in several other places in his epistles as well. You see, the nations of the world are blessed in Abraham because all those who accept the gospel of salvation are grafted into the nation of Israel through faith in Yeshua, and they become joint heirs with Israel. They become sons and daughters of the living God. They are born again not of blood, nor of the will of the flesh nor of the will of man, but of God. They are adopted into the family of God. They become one with the Lord, one with the Father, and one with Israel. They become Israelites. They do not become Jews, for one must be born a Jew to be a Jew, but they are grafted into Israel. Therefore, they become Israelites. So it is that the gospel of salvation is a vital part of the gospel of the kingdom so that both the redemption and the restoration of Israel will be fulfilled. Of course, you realize, my son, that we are speaking of these things on a very simplistic level."

"Yes, I understand. I am just so grateful that the Lord of the mountain is pleased to share these things with me. I am also grateful to you, Solomon, for being a willing vessel for Him to do so." I continued, "Solomon, there are Jewish people living in the land today. They have come from my side of the mountain and returned to your side of the mountain. They have also come from the beach and from the sea. Is that what you mean by bringing them back from the nations of the world?" I asked.

"Let's look back and allow history to speak to us. We have briefly discussed this, but it is needful to revisit it for more clarity and understanding. After the death of King David's son, Solomon, Israel was divided into two kingdoms. One was the Northern Kingdom consisting of ten tribes and was also known as Ephraim because Ephraim was the largest tribe. The other was the Southern Kingdom consisting of two tribes: Judah and Benjamin. The Southern Kingdom was also known as Judah because Judah was the largest tribe. Look here at the ancient map and you will see that Ephraim occupied northern Israel while Judah occupied southern Israel including Jerusalem, the city of David."

"Oh, that's why the prophets speak to Ephraim sometimes and at other times to Judah," I stated.

"Exactly!" he responded. "Shortly after the kingdom was divided, the Northern Kingdom began worshiping false gods, refusing to honor the God of Israel. God judged them. The Assyrian Empire defeated them and, as was their custom, dispersed Ephraim into other nations where they could no longer regather and become a future threat. While exiled within these nations, they no longer practiced their religion or acknowledged the covenant with Abraham. They would become as those among whom they lived. They assimilated themselves into the customs of the nations where they were driven, thus losing their identity as Israelites. The God of Israel was, therefore, keeping the terms of His covenant. He had said that if they did not keep His statutes and commandments they would be cursed. However, God would remain faithful to the covenant promises and planned to bring them back to the land. Do you know how He would do that, James?"

"Yes, I remember you saying that it was through the preaching of the gospel of salvation to the nations in which they had been scattered. The disciples of Yeshua went out as fishers of men."

"Yes, that's right James. Do you see in this the tremendous plan of God? He would punish the people by tearing the family apart while all the time using this punishment as a way to bless the nations, just as He had promised to Abraham when He said, 'In you will all the nations of the world be blessed.'"

"But how were the nations blessed?" I asked.

"They were blessed because as the disciples were sent to the lost sheep of the house of Israel within the nations, the gospel of salvation was preached. All those who heard it, though not descendants of Abraham, Isaac, and Jacob, could be grafted into Israel by receiving the gospel of salvation."

"I never saw that before! Our God is truly amazing."

"Yes, and He is faithful to keep His promises. You see, Yeshua did not come to erase the past by starting over with making a new covenant with others outside of Israel. He came to fulfill that covenant made with Abraham and his descendants, which is the everlasting covenant. In fulfilling His covenant, He reached out to all the people of every nation offering to graft them into the nation of Israel, to become one people through the blood atonement of Yeshua. That is why the Apostle Paul says with confidence, 'All Israel will be saved.' He is assured of this from what the Prophet Isaiah had prophesied."

I was amazed at all that Solomon had shared with me, but I had one question. I wasn't sure how to phrase it. I didn't want it to seem as if I was disrespecting the Lord. I decided there was no other way to state it, so I said, "Solomon, God's plan is certainly great, but why isn't it working?"

"Do you mean why is there this great gulf between the Jews on my side of the mountain and the Christians on your side of the mountain?" he asked.

"Exactly. The two are definitely not one family."

"That, my son, is the question of the age, and we shall approach that question in our next discussion. I am tired now and I still have my evening prayers."

"All right," I said, "but it will be hard to sleep with that question on my mind."

"Pray for a dream tonight and perhaps the Lord will use it to speak to you."

I left Solomon in his study, went to the kitchen, grabbed a snack, and headed up to my room.

CHAPTER 10

Honoring the Sabbath

I NOTICED IT WAS quite chilly when I got out of bed the next morning. I had awakened earlier than usual, and I didn't hear Solomon in the kitchen. Stepping into the hall I saw that his bedroom door was still closed, so I assumed that he wasn't up yet. The hallway was extremely cold, so I went downstairs to check on the wood stove. It hadn't been started nor was there any wood in the house. I quietly went back upstairs and got dressed, then went outside to gather some wood. After bringing in all the wood that the wood box near the stove would hold, I got some kindling and started the fire. It wasn't long before the cabin was nice and cozy warm. I hadn't noticed Solomon come down and could hear him in his study going through his morning prayers. The sun had come up and things were brightening outside. I went out onto the porch and moved Solomon's chair into the sunlight, sat down and began rocking and enjoying the warmth of the sun. I soon heard the familiar sound of pots and pans and knew Solomon was preparing breakfast. I thought about revisiting the stream after breakfast, but I wasn't sure what Solomon had in mind for the day. Not much time had gone by when I heard a tap on the window and turned to see Solomon motioning me to come in. I went inside, and he asked me to give thanks and to pray for the day. After praying, we sat down to enjoy the first meal of the day. I asked him if he needed me for anything.

He said, "The Sabbath begins tonight." I waited for a follow up to that statement, but he simply continued eating.

Finally, he asked, "What do you know about the Sabbath?"

"I know that it is celebrated on one side of the mountain and not on the other."

"Why do you suppose that is?" he asked.

"I think it is because on my side of the mountain they choose to celebrate the resurrection of our Lord as the day of assembly and worship."

"Who decided?" he asked in a demanding voice.

"The Christians," I said. Suddenly I felt like I was being interrogated. He usually looked me in the eye when we conversed, but now he was picking up pieces of food with his fork and examining them while he asked me questions. After putting the food in his mouth, he looked down at his plate while chewing, awaiting my response. Once his mouth was empty he would ask another question.

"Did Yeshua tell them to change the day of worship?"

"I don't think so?"

"Did Yeshua honor the Sabbath Day?"

"Of course, He did. He was Jewish."

"Is He then only the Lord of the Jews?"

"No, He is the Lord of all who believe in Him. He's their Savior and Lord."

"Yes, and did He not say if you love Me, you will keep My commandments? And are we not told that as disciples we must walk in His ways, walk as He walked? Is a disciple greater than his master?"

All these things came rolling out of his mouth one after the other.

"He did say those things, and no, a disciple is not greater than his master," I replied.

"Is the honoring of the Sabbath a commandment?" he continued.

"Yes, it is. It is the fourth commandment," I replied.

"Then who authorized this change to the commandment of God?"

"I don't know. The church fathers I guess."

"You see, my son, we have a problem when the church fathers or the Jewish religious leaders or anyone else adds or takes away from the Word of God. It then becomes mixed. Mixture brings about confusion, and the enemy of our souls uses mixture to separate the things that God wants joined together. A mixture is created when what our Lord says is right and then man adds or takes away from it, something that we will discuss more at a later time." His tone changed, and it felt like he had finally ended the interrogation.

"You're saying we should be keeping the Sabbath on both sides of the mountain."

"Yes, unless you can show me where the Lord of the mountain has changed His mind."

We finished breakfast and I cleared off the table and did the dishes while Solomon returned to his study. I then returned to the rocking chair on the porch to enjoy more of the sun all the while thinking about what had just taken place at the kitchen table. Maybe Solomon woke up on the wrong side of the bed. After all, he did sleep in a little later than other mornings—so much so that the fire had gone out in the wood stove. It's just like when the church sleeps, I thought, the fire of the Lord goes out. Oh boy, I thought, now I'm thinking like Solomon. A dull ax and a sleeping church won't get much done in either case.

I went upstairs to get my Bible, so I could read some passages having to do with the Sabbath. About an hour later, Solomon came out to join me on the porch. When he noticed the opened Bible in my lap, he asked what I was reading. I told him that I was looking at passages concerning the Sabbath. He went to sit down on the step and I quickly offered him the chair, but he refused my offer and sat on the step.

"May I ask you a question, Solomon?"

"Of course," he said. "I will not always have the answer to your questions, but I am willing to give you all that I have."

"People didn't honor the Sabbath until after they came out of Egypt, when it was instituted through Moses. Is that correct?" I asked.

"No, James, that is not correct. The Sabbath was instituted during the creation. Do you remember that it is written in Genesis 2:2-3: 'And on the seventh day God ended His work which He had made; and He rested on the seventh day from all His work which He had made. And God blessed the seventh day and sanctified it: because that in it He had rested from all His work which God created and made.' James, we are told here that God blessed the seventh day and sanctified it. He told Adam and Eve to tend the Garden, but they were to rest on the Sabbath just as He did. The Sabbath was made for man, and from the beginning it was to be honored."

"Why does it go from sunset to sunset and not midnight to midnight like all the other days?" I inquired.

Solomon then took the time to explain to me that a biblical day begins in the evening. He said that we understand this from the creation account as well. We are told that the beginning of time was marked by darkness. "The earth was without form and void, and darkness was over the face of the deep." Solomon then took my Bible and opened it up to Genesis 1 pointing out that it goes on to tell us that the days of the week were originally measured from evening to morning. There was evening and there was morning the first day, there was evening and there was morning the second day, and so on. Solomon then said, "James, since we are on this subject, may I share with you what else we learn from this seven-day account of creation?"

"Sure," I said.

"Then let's go to the study where I can make use of some books." I got up from the rocker and followed him into the study where Solomon began pulling a few books off the shelves and then set them on his desk.

CHAPTER 11

The Seven Thousand Year Plan

SOLOMON ONCE AGAIN DIRECTED me to bring my chair over to the desk.

"Put it where you sat last time so that we can look on together."

He continued, "It is believed by our people on my side of the mountain that the Creator of the universe, knowing full well that mankind would sin and need redemption, had planned the way of redemption from before the foundation of the world. The Apostle Paul speaks of this in his opening statement to the church at Ephesus. Then Moses tells us that a thousand years in His sight is like yesterday when it is past. Also, the Apostle Peter wrote that one day is as a thousand years, and a thousand years as one day with our God. We believe this to be a biblical principle.

What the Creator of the universe is telling us in His account of the creation of the earth and man is that at the end of six days, or six thousand years, there would be a day of rest, a Sabbath rest for one thousand years. This Sabbath period is when Yeshua will rule and reign on the earth from Jerusalem. Let me show you the time line described in this book on the plan of salvation. Or, if you prefer, we could go to the genealogy of Jesus Christ in the first chapter of Matthew and also in Luke chapter three. But for now, let's look in this book on God's plan of salvation and how it is presented to us here.

From Adam to Abraham	1,948 years
Abraham to Egypt	290 years
From Egypt to Moses	63 years
From Moses to the Exodus	80 years
From Exodus to death of Joshua	70 years
From Judges to Samuel	450 years
Kings of Judah	513 years
Babylonian Captivity	586 years
Adam to Yeshua	4,000 years

Thus, you have here the first four days, or the first four thousand years, of the Creator's plan of salvation. During this time, God made covenants with His chosen people and He instructed them through the Torah, the first five books of the TaNaKh, the Bible. From the time of Yeshua's first coming to His second coming would be another two days, or another two thousand years, bringing us to a total of six thousand years. These are all six days or years of labor. The seventh day brings Yeshua's return, and with it a Sabbath rest of one thousand years while He rules and reigns upon the earth from Jerusalem. This is why you are here, James. This is why there is so much activity upon the mountain, on both sides of the mountain today. We may be entering or already have entered the seventh day. Yeshua told us that no man knows the day or the hour, but that we must be watchful and ready. We are to recognize the *season* of His return. With this in mind, we must once again discuss Yeshua's mission, why He came to the earth the first time and why He will come again. However, I know that you wanted to visit the stream today, so you should go as I prepare for the Sabbath. We will pick up with our conversation this evening.

I walked down to the stream and found my tree. As I sat down and began listening to the stream, I was still thinking about the last thing Solomon had said, "We may be entering, or have entered, the seventh day." I remembered how distorted things had gotten on the other side of the mountain—at least that was my perception. It was difficult to watch all the people from the sea coming onto the mountain and all of the compromise they brought into the various camps upon the mountain. Most of them did not come up using the trodden path, where they would first stop at the Tree of Life and be reborn. Instead, they were forging their own way up the mountain and entering the camps from strange new paths. It was as if a kind of darkness was settling upon the mountain.

It seemed to me that the light that once had shown so brightly and had made an evident distinction in the way that those who dwelt on the mountain lived out their lives from those who lived on the sea was fading, was being shut out. There was at first a subtle merging of ways and then an *obvious* merging of ways. Once we got high enough up the mountain, things seemed a bit clearer, and then finding this valley, well, that was like walking into an oasis. Then finding Solomon was like entering a whole new world. I now felt totally separated from the darkness. I then remembered the warning given by the shepherd in the settlement. Was I being deceived? Every conversation seemed to bring such a fresh perspective. Things that were so puzzling before, those things they called "the mysteries" on my side of the mountain, now didn't seem so mysterious. Everything in the Bible began to come together for me.

My thoughts went back to the compromising on my side of the mountain that had brought darkness to the mountain. How could we possibly be entering into the seventh day, the reign of Yeshua on the earth. That would not bring darkness, it would bring tremendous light. It would be the glory of the Lord in the earth. Then that familiar voice again, "The day begins with darkness, there was darkness then there was light, the seventh day." Oh wow!" I thought. Here is another conversation with Solomon. Then I prayed, "Lord please give me understanding. Help me to discern the truth of

Your Word. Lead me and guide me and keep me from deception. I ask this of You, Heavenly Father in the name of Yeshua. Amen"

I rose to my feet and began heading back to the cabin. I really wanted this issue to be our conversation for tonight, but I knew that Solomon had already said that we would converse on the mission of Yeshua and why He came to earth and is returning. Perhaps one topic would lead into the other as so often seemed to be the case.

CHAPTER 12

The Mission of Yeshua

THE MEAL TOOK MUCH longer that evening because it was the Sabbath. I had learned to enjoy the Sabbath meal, but I was very anxious to get to the conversation. I wanted to bring it up during the meal, but Solomon didn't like me doing that even when it wasn't the Sabbath, and there really was no time during the Sabbath meal due to the Torah readings that accompanied the meal. It would have to wait. Once the meal had ended and the candle had been extinguished, then finally we could begin our conversation, or at least I thought we could. Solomon informed me otherwise by asking me if I played an instrument. I said, "Yes I play the guitar and a little piano."

He said, "I have both. Which do you prefer?"

"Well, I'm better at the guitar."

"Wonderful! I will go to my room and get the guitar. You decide what song you will teach me this evening and then we can worship together and delight in the Lord of the Sabbath."

"Are we not going to have our conversation tonight," I asked?

"Yes, but first we worship." He went up the stairs and quickly returned with a very nice guitar. I was surprised he would have such an instrument. He handed it to me and began to dance his way over to the chair across the sitting room. He was more joyful than I had ever seen him. It was a child-like joy that filled him.

"I will teach you two songs," I said. "One is a very simple song that the Chief Musician gave to me early on in my climb and the other is one of my favorite worship songs."

"So, you call our Lord the Chief Musician?" he asked.

"Yes, actually both the Lord and the Holy Spirit. When I first came to know Him, He filled me with music and everything around me was full of music, and I knew that He, the Lord together with the Holy Spirit, was conducting it all."

"Wonderful!" he shouted. Wow! Two wonderfuls in a row, I thought to myself. "You play and sing and when I feel I know it, I will join in," he said.

"Well, the song I want to play for you first is not really a song that we can sing together. I would like you to just sit and maybe close your eyes and listen to the words. Then I will teach you a song from the Scriptures that you may already know. If you don't know the song, you will certainly recognize the Scripture. Is that okay?"

"Yes", he said. "I will sit and listen to your song."

I sang:

> We see His beauty in our ashes, feel wonder
> with the rain.
> Hear His glory in the thunder, find His mercy
> in our pain,
> And as we journey onward, through this veil of tears,
> We hear His voice relentlessly, through the agony
> and ecstasy.
> I'm alive, and I'm coming for you!
> I will hide you away in the coming storm,
> As the kingdoms rage and the peoples mourn.
> I'm alive, and I'm coming for you.
> The One who rose from the dead, having all authority,
> Stores our tears in a bottle and throws our sins
> into the sea.
> He will read our names, from the Book of Life
> Feed us with His hidden manna, during times of strife.
> I'm alive, and the night will be rolled away,
> The times of Jacob's Trouble will surely end one day.
> Wait, with watchful eyes and known that I will come.
> Hope in My promise of rest, when all is said and done.

I'm alive, and I'm coming for you!
I will hide you away in the coming storm,
As the kingdoms rage and the peoples mourn.
I'm alive, and I'm coming for you.

"Ah yes," Solomon said. "You are singing of the times of Jacob's Trouble, what you call the tribulation period on your side of the mountain."

"Yes," I said. "There is a growing conversation about the tribulation on my side of the mountain. It began several years ago, but it always seems to get pushed aside, and though there is a great deal of conversation about it, we never seem to come to a conclusion on what it will bring or when it might be. So I was sitting by the stream one day and praying about it and this song began to run through my head."

"We will discuss this at some point and see if we can find answers to your questions regarding this issue," Solomon said, obviously brushing aside any discussion of it now. Then he quickly said, "Now what is this song from the Scriptures you want to share with me?"

I picked up the guitar again and began to play the chords to the song. "It is a song we sing on my side of the mountain and it is taken from Isaiah 6," I said as I began to sing the song. Suddenly, I heard a loud exuberant voice coming from the other side of the room. He knew the song all right. I lifted my voice to try and match the intensity with which he was singing to the Lord, and we sang the song perhaps six or seven times. Solomon stood and raised his arms to the Lord, rejoicing in the joy of the Lord as he sang.

Our singing faded and became a time of intercession, and we found ourselves praying for both sides of the mountain intensely and sincerely. Then Solomon said, "Perhaps we should begin our discussion concerning the Messiah."

"Yes, I am looking forward to this conversation."

"Then let's enter the study," he suggested. "By the way, James, I enjoyed worshiping our Savior with you. We must do it again soon."

"I look forward to that," I said.

"Yes, and I will teach you a song or two from my side of the mountain." He went to his desk and I retrieved the chair and positioned it where I had sat before without waiting to be directed.

"Now," he said, "we said that we would discuss why it was that Yeshua came to earth. Let me begin by stating what we have already agreed upon since your arrival. We know that everything has to do with covenant and that these covenants are everlasting so that a new or renewed covenant simply adds to the previous covenant. We also know that the only nation that the God of Israel ever made a covenant of salvation and restoration with was Israel, including the new or renewed covenant. We know that Israel is the name that was given to Jacob and that from Jacob/Israel came twelve sons, which became known as the twelve tribes of Israel. We also know that Joseph had two sons while in Egypt and that Jacob, when he went to Egypt, blessed these two sons and, in a sense, adopted them, giving them an inheritance in what was to become the nation of Israel. We have also seen from the Scriptures that Yeshua came for the lost sheep of the house of Israel and sent out fishers to fish them out of the nations in accordance to the prophetic promise. Am I right in stating that we agree on these things, James?"

"Yes, although as you have said many times we have only lightly touched upon these things, and so I still do have a great deal of questions."

"That is fine, James. These things that we have just listed are the pieces that are necessary for us to understand the mission of Yeshua and why He came to earth. It is also important that these things are all found and confirmed in the Scriptures.

Now, as to the first point and its relationship to His coming to earth, one of the very first covenants Yeshua made was with Adam and Eve. After they sinned they were told that a son would be born from the seed of Eve and that He would crush the head of the serpent who had led her into deception and ultimately into sin. So it is this covenant that began the process of salvation and restoration."

"But we just agreed that Israel was the only nation that God ever made a covenant of salvation and restoration with," I stated.

"That is true, James. Adam and Eve were not a nation." He informed me.

"Oh, yes, that's true." I said.

"Every succeeding covenant has to do with this initial covenant made as the two exited Eden. Future covenants would either focus on further defining how it would come about or what was needed to prepare the people for this redemption and restoration. So you see, James, the fulfillment of covenant promises made by God is the mission of the Messiah and why He came to earth the first time, and it will be why He comes to earth the second time. He is that seed of Eve."

"Yes, I can see that," I said.

"Now, if we were to take the time to really examine all seven covenants from the fall of man to the full redemption of man, and the progression of revelation within each covenant, we would have a pretty clear understanding of why Yeshua came and why He said what He said and did what He did while upon the earth. There is a definite correlation to what He said and did and the covenant language found within the covenants themselves.

As to the second point, the nation of Israel being the only nation that the Lord ever covenanted with, has to do with what is called the *echad* of God, meaning the oneness of God. I'm sure you have read the passage in Deuteronomy where He declares to Israel, 'Hear, O Israel: The LORD our God, the LORD is one!' This is a declaration of the *echad* of God. It establishes that God, His Word, and Israel are all one. This was the basis for Yeshua's prayer in John 17, where He stated the desire of the Father that they should be one even as He and the Father were one. We also understand from the Scriptures that Israel is to be the nation that is to bring Torah to the other nations of the world. Yeshua is the living Word and the Word is the Torah, so Yeshua is the Living Torah. This brings us to another part of the mission of God. He came to earth to declare His Father's will to Israel and thus to the world. The Apostle John tells us that the 'Word [Torah] became flesh and dwelt among us.' He came to 'fulfill the law and the prophets.' The word *law* is synonymous with the word *Torah.* The Torah contains the law, but its real meaning is 'instruction.' To *fulfill* in this passage means to 'fully explain or reveal its intended meaning'.

"Do you remember James, when I told you that we often need to go back to the original language to get a clear understanding of what is being communicated?"

"Yes, I do remember, and if from the original language we understand that Torah means instruction, then it really does take on a whole new meaning. I would much rather have instruction than law. I think anybody would. And if to *fulfill* means to 'fully explain,' then Yeshua's words have a value that I never understood before. I mean, if He came to clarify for me, for us, what the prophets and the Torah are saying, then I need to look at His words again."

"Oh, and James, we have already mentioned this, but it is of such great importance to understanding His mission that I must repeat it. The only way one, anyone, can be saved is by being grafted into redeemed Israel through Yeshua the Savior, because it is only with Israel that God has covenanted.

"As to the other points that we have listed, they have to do with the history of Israel. The history of Israel is where we find the covenants of God, and the events that foreshadow things yet to take place. We also understand the relationship between God and His people where He is identified as the Good Shepherd of Israel whose mission it was to come to find the lost sheep of the house of Israel. Do you think that you can now define the mission of Yeshua in coming to earth?"

"I'm sure that I have much more to learn, but I certainly could give a more thorough definition than I could before coming here. Before our time together, I simply would have quoted John 3:16 to answer that question. Now I can say with confidence that He came to fulfill the covenant promises made to Abraham and all the other patriarchs, including the promise to gather the lost sheep of Israel from the nations where they have been exiled and to reunite the two houses of Israel. I now know that all who believe in Yeshua from among the nations of the world are grafted into Israel. The two sides of the mountain are becoming more clearly associated than I had ever seen before."

CHAPTER 13

The Lord Is My Shepherd

WE FINISHED UP FOR the night and both headed upstairs to bed. That night I dreamed of sheep. When I awoke, the dream was on my mind and so I lay there reviewing it in my mind. I wondered why God chose to use the metaphor of a shepherd and sheep. Of course, this led me to grab my Bible on the nightstand and open to Psalm 23. I was always comforted by this psalm. It is such a personal psalm. He is our Shepherd and He tends to our needs like a shepherd tends to the needs of his sheep. I read through the psalm and then lay my head on my pillow and began to give thanks to Yeshua. Then I heard His voice. He said, "Read the psalm again and think of Israel." I thought that was strange, but I wanted to be obedient if it was the Lord. As I read verses one through three thinking of Israel, I could see that it was true for Israel. The Lord is Israel's Shepherd. They lack nothing when they are in His pasture. He did make them to lie down in green pastures and lead them beside the still waters. He led them into the promised land. He often would restore her soul. When she had departed and left the sheep fold, He brought her back. He certainly leads her in the paths of righteousness for His name's sake. I sat up in bed with a greater interest in reading the rest of the psalm now. Israel, like no other nation on earth, has walked through the valley of the shadow of death. When they trusted in God, they did not fear any evil. They knew from their history and the Torah and prophets that God was greater than any evil. He was with them. He said that He would never leave them nor forsake them. He comforts them with His rod and His staff. They were comforted to know that He would come with His shepherd's staff to bring them back should they wander off. This was the great hope they had as they now climbed the mountain. I read the rest of the psalm and could see every line fitting the history, the relationship with the Shepherd, and even the future of Israel.

I set my Bible down beside me on the bed and lay back down to consider why the Lord would show me this concerning Israel. Then it occurred to me. I am grafted into Israel and so this is personal to me as an Israelite. I smiled and thought, how wonderful the Lord is. Then I heard Him speak once more. "Read the psalm again and think of Me." I immediately sat up, grabbed my Bible, and began to read with the Lord in mind. "The LORD is my shepherd." Now, I understood it to be the Lord speaking of His Father. It was becoming so clear.

This could certainly be the Lord when He would be here on earth. Was David being given a glimpse of the Lord in His earthly ministry before He ever came to earth, or was He prophesying what His earthly ministry would be like? He did say that He came for the sake of His Father's name. Who knew more about walking through the valley of the shadow of death? With great assurance He could say, "And I will dwell in the house of the LORD Forever." Amazingly, He was confirming what Solomon had taught me about the *echad* of God. The Father, the Son, the Holy Spirit, and Israel could all be seen in this one psalm that I always thought was just a psalm of comfort for David and for each of us who read it. I was beginning to see that Scripture, especially prophetic Scriptures, could have more than one meaning, just like historical events were often prophetic of future events. I couldn't wait to share this with Solomon. Now, finally I had something I could offer as a part of the conversation. I decided that this time I wasn't going to rush to get my thoughts heard. I would enjoy breakfast with him and invite him to sit out on the porch with me and then I would share my dream and how the Lord gave me a greater understanding of *echad*.

I got up and got ready for the day. By the time I was ready to leave my room, I could smell breakfast. I went downstairs and greeted Solomon and then sat down at the table. He turned from the stove and walked to the table with the frying pan in hand and filled my plate. We bowed our heads and asked the Lord's blessing on the day.

When we had finished eating and while I was cleaning up, I thought about how to begin the conversation. I would start by saying, Solomon, I have something to share with you about the *echad* of God. Just then, I heard the Lord say, "I have been given something to share." I said under my breath, "Yes Lord, I'm sorry. I know it was you who gave this to me and that we have nothing that has not been given to us." I knew that the Lord was not just looking for the credit. He was teaching me that it is important that when we offer spiritual things we must tie them back to Him. By stating that, I had been given something to share, I acknowledged it came from the Lord. If someone didn't understand, they would ask, "given by whom?" Then I would say, "By the Lord." It ties back to Him either way. "Thank you again, Lord," I said.

CHAPTER 14

The Visit

When I had finished in the kitchen, I went looking for Solomon. I called to him from the bottom of the stairs.

"Solomon, are you up there?"

"No, I'm in my study," he called back. I went to his study, and as I was about to enter, he opened the door and stood there with his hat on and a briefcase in his hand.

"Are you going somewhere?" I asked.

"Yes," he replied. "I am going to my friend's house on my side of the mountain. You met him. He was one of the two men who brought the supplies last week." "Oh," I said. "I will be back in a few days. I'm afraid that you will have to do your own cooking while I'm away. You know where everything is. Do you think that you can handle that, James?"

"Of course," I responded.

"Good, then I will see you in a few days." I watched him walk out the door wondering why he hadn't told me he was going, as well as, wondering why he was going. I watched him through the window until he disappeared from sight all the while talking with the Lord and asking Him what I was supposed to do now. He would be gone for a few days, and I had been wondering from time to time how things were going back at the settlement. It didn't take me long to decide that I would take this opportunity to go back to the settlement to see how things were there. I quickly went upstairs to my room, gathered a few things I thought I may need, including my Bible, and then headed out the door. I was only a few feet from the cabin when I thought, I need to go back and leave a note on the table, just in case he arrives back before I do. So I returned to the cabin, sat at the kitchen table and wrote him a note: "Solomon, I have taken this opportunity while you are away to return to the settlement to see how things are with my companions. I will return soon to finish our conversation. God bless you, James." Then I headed out again in the direction of the settlement.

Upon arriving at the settlement, I was greeted by some of those I had met before I left. They seemed excited to see me. I asked them if my companions were still in the settlement.

"Oh, yes," one of them quickly replied. "We have been praying for your return ever since you left."

"Why were you praying for my return?" I asked.

"We were instructed by the shepherds to pray for you while you were at the cabin," he answered.

I thought that was interesting. It wasn't so much as what he said, but the way he said it. Praise God, I'll take prayer any time I can get it. The Lord knows I need it. I quickly found my companions and we enjoyed a nice reunion. They were all excited about continuing on with our journey up the mountain.

"James, we can start gathering some supplies together tomorrow and then make plans to start up again," one of the men suggested.

"I'm really sorry, but I'm not finished with my time at the cabin. I just came to see how you were doing. I plan on heading back to the cabin in a couple of days."

You could have heard a pin drop in that room. They all looked at me and then began looking at each other. Finally, one of them said, "Why are you going back? What is it that you are doing there?"

"I'm learning," I said, "about the history and ways on the other side of the mountain."

They began to respond to my statement one after another and even some together at the same time: "Why are you learning about the other side of the mountain?" "Didn't the shepherd warn you about becoming confused?" "Are you going to finish your climb on the other side of the mountain?" "What are we supposed to do?"

"I'll answer all of your questions as best I can and explain what I'm doing after dinner tonight," I said. They quieted down and began talking amongst themselves.

We asked to use one of the halls in the settlement to have our meeting that evening. After grabbing a cup of coffee, we sat around a large table in the hall. Then, I began sharing with them about the conversations I had been having with Solomon. I shared how I had grown to really appreciate Solomon, who was a kind and gentle man. I told them how, in just a few weeks, I had come to have very high regard for him. As to the warning of the shepherd upon my departure, I did not feel that Solomon was a threat in any way. Did he have differing views as to how one should climb the mountain? Absolutely. Were they informative or were they destructive to the views I held during my entire climb up the mountain? I explained that they added to my knowledge and brought clarity to so many things I had previously thought I understood. I told them I felt I had gained an understanding of why there are the two sides to the mountain, meaning a separation between our climb and theirs. I also told them that I believed, for the first time, that we could and must help each other to reach the top of the mountain.

The very next day one of the shepherds in the settlement asked if he could have a word with me. He then began the conversation by stating I had unsettled some of the companions who had traveled with me to the settlement. He said that a few of them came to him earlier and told him about the meeting that was held the night before. They were very concerned about some of the things I had shared. He then added his concern about me sharing these things with the people in the settlement. He didn't want them to become confused. He didn't want me to disturb the harmony in their settlement. He never asked me what it was that Solomon had shared or what I had shared at the meeting. He only wanted me not to speak of those things again while in the settlement. Respecting the fact that he was the authority in the settlement, I agreed to his request. We parted ways, and I wondered who as well as how many of my companions were disturbed. I was saddened by the conversation with the shepherd. I guess I had hoped by coming back to the settlement I could create some kind of bridge between Solomon and the shepherds, although I don't remember ever determining to do that. I felt bad that I had brought discord into the camp. There was now a mistrust between me and my companions, and I felt unwelcomed.

As I went about the settlement I realized that people were looking at me with suspicion and everyone I had to do with that day was just trying to be gracious. I sought out one of the shepherds to ask him what it was that was so disturbing about my connection with Solomon. I soon found one of the shepherds and asked if I could have a word with him.

He politely said, "Yes, I would love to."

"Could you please tell me what is so threatening about my connection with Solomon?" I asked.

"I and some of the other shepherds have met with Solomon on occasion. He is a nice enough man, but what he wants to do is lead people back under the law. Jesus' death on the cross has set us free from the law," he stated.

"He has never once mentioned the law to me in all of our conversations," I rebutted.

"No, he calls it the Torah, but if you look at the Torah, it's all about law. We're responsible for guarding God's people from returning to something His Son died to free us from," he said.

"I see," I said. "But, he believes that Yeshua, Jesus, is the Messiah."

"Yes, I know he does. It's all that other stuff that would put the people in bondage, or at the very least, confuse and discourage them," he said.

We ended our conversation and parted ways.

I didn't sleep much that night knowing I had a decision to make that would drastically change my life. I tossed and turned and wrestled with trying to understand what it was the Lord wanted me to do. It was His will that I was most concerned about not mine. I knew I could adjust and make it in either world, but I wanted to do what the Lord of the mountain wanted me to do. How could I know for sure what His will was for me?

The next morning, I was greeted by one of my companions. He came to tell me that the group had decided to leave the settlement and continue their climb up the mountain. He wanted to know if I would be accompanying them. They had held a brief meeting earlier that morning to discuss whether or not they should appoint someone new to lead the way. They did appoint someone to replace me, but he stated that they would nonetheless be pleased if I would join them. I said that I would inform them of my decision after a time of prayer.

I skipped breakfast and went just outside the settlement into a field to pray. As I prayed I looked down the valley at the log cabin. I closed my eyes and put my face in my hands and began to cry out to the Lord. "Lord, please show me what you want me to do. It's like there is no right or wrong answer here. We are all Your people. I just need to know what you want me to do."

It was then that I heard His voice. "Look up," He said.

I looked up and what I saw, a little way in front of me, were three deer walking from the woods into the valley. I was sure it was the mother and her two fawns that I had seen at the stream. I had my answer. I was to return to the cabin and to family, or at least to where the understanding of family was being cultivated.

"Thank you, Lord," I said over and over again.

I returned to the settlement to say goodbye to my companions. They were not all together so I found as many of them as I could and explained that I would be returning to the cabin. I prayed with each one, asking the Lord's blessing on their climb. It was approaching noon, and I needed to leave soon in order to reach the cabin by nightfall. I gathered the few things that I had brought with me and headed out. It felt like I was going home. I so hoped that Solomon would be there when I arrived.

As I walked along, I started thinking about the last conversation I had with the shepherd. I truly didn't remember Solomon ever talking about the law, but he did talk a great deal about the Torah and many of the references to covenant were in the Torah. I knew that I would have to ask him about his past conversations with the shepherds that would lead them to think he was trying to lead them back to the law. Oh wait, I thought. He did mention the law in one of our conversations. We were talking about the statement Yeshua made about coming to fulfill the law. I didn't remember that conversation as having to do with being under the law. I remembered it had more to do with the Torah being instruction. I would have to ask Solomon to clarify these things for me.

All of a sudden, I saw smoke rising from the cabin. Ah, Solomon is home. I picked up the pace. I was a little hungry and hoped that he was making enough dinner for the two of us, but he probably wouldn't be, not knowing when I would be home. I could just whip up something for myself. Suddenly thoughts began to fill my head that made me feel very unsettled. I began to wonder if Solomon had left hoping that I would leave in his absence. Maybe he didn't want me around anymore. Was I just assuming that he wanted me to stay? Had we finished our conversation? Had I overstayed my welcome? If he didn't want me to stay, where would I go? I suppose I could go in pursuit of my companions, but that didn't appear to be what the Lord was indicating I should do. I stopped and sat down on the grass and began to pray.

"Lord, I need to know what you want me to do. You have always been faithful to guide me, but now I'm not sure about anything. Just a few days ago, before Solomon left and I returned to the settlement, I felt more complete than ever. I felt that I was learning more about Your ways and Your will for those climbing the mountain, pursuing the high places. Now Lord, I'm just not sure which way to turn."

I looked up to see where the sun was, trying to determine how much time I had before darkness fell. There was a cloud formation just above me. It appeared to be a large shepherd's staff. While looking at it, the words of David came to me. "The Lord is my shepherd, I shall not want." Then I heard the words of the Lord follow, "I am the shepherd of your soul. I lead you to green pastures. Continue on and I will be with you."

I could not contain the emotion within, and I began to weep. As I wept, I realized that what had taken place at the settlement had wounded me. The doubt I had entertained about Solomon's welcome had dampened my hope. Now, I knew that the Lord was healing my wound and dispelling my doubt by using His Word. His word became living and active within me and was separating soul and spirit.

He had said, "Continue on and I will be with you." That was all I needed to hear. I stood to my feet, wiped the tears from my face, and headed toward the cabin.

CHAPTER 15

Home Again

As soon as my feet hit the porch, Solomon was out with an embrace.

"It is good to see you, James," he said. "We have both arrived home within hours of each other."

Oh, that welcome was exactly what I needed.

"Come in and we can have dinner together. I have been so used to cooking for two that I automatically cooked for two this evening. There is plenty."

I felt so at home. I remembered during my climb up the mountain I had entered dozens of camps, but I had never really felt at home in any of them. I was thankful for the many wonderful people I had met whose lives were given to serving the Lord and to ascending the mountain. I just never felt as at home as I did here in this cabin. How difficult it was going to be when it would come time to leave. However, I need to live for the present and enjoy the time we had left together, I thought. I remembered how the Lord wants us to be anxious for nothing and told us in Scripture to consider the lilies of the field and the birds of the air and to seek first the kingdom of God and all we need will be given to us. I sat down at the table and we prayed, giving thanks for a safe return to the cabin and for His provision, then we ate our meal.

Solomon never spoke about his days when he was gone from the cabin, and I never asked. I just figured if he wanted to tell me, he would. I, on the other hand, needed to talk with him about what had taken place at the settlement and especially about the issue of being brought back under the law. He didn't ask me about my visit that evening, but I would look for the right time to open that conversation. The rest of the evening Solomon spent in his study. I went up to my room and lay on my bed reading until I fell asleep.

I awoke the next morning still fully dressed with the open book beside me on the bed. The sun was just coming up. As it rose it shone through the clouds that hid the top of the mountain making it appear like there was some kind of glorious place beyond the clouds. I was certain there was. I moved from my bed to the chair where I could look out the window and get a better view while I began a time of prayer and thanksgiving. I could hear Solomon already downstairs. It sounded like he was sweeping up around the wood stove where the wood was stacked. Bringing the wood in and stacking it by the stove made quite a mess, and he was really fussy about keeping it clean. I wondered if I should check out back to see if more wood needed to be split. Then I thought, no, we had both been gone so there would probably still be plenty. I sat there looking out the window at the landscape around the cabin. I located a place that I thought would be great for a vegetable garden. That would be something where I could contribute. Then it occurred to me that I had no idea how long I would be staying here. I shouldn't make any long-term plans like that. I shouldn't get too settled. That was contrary to what the Lord had said was my destiny. I was to continue to climb the mountain and, at some point, I knew it would be necessary. I stopped my musing, got up and began getting ready for the day. I knew Solomon would start cooking breakfast soon.

CHAPTER 16

The Law

WE FINISHED BREAKFAST AND once again Solomon headed into his study for morning prayers while I cleaned up in the kitchen. More wood needed to be brought in, so I took care of that task. I was either going to go back to my room to read or bring my book and read out on the porch. What I really wanted to do was talk with Solomon about the shepherds in the settlement. I was getting a little anxious about it and wanted to get it over with. Solomon and I had not had one disagreement since I came here. I didn't want this anticipated discussion to end in disagreement. I remembered that Solomon had previously laid the ground rules for our discussions early on in our first conversation. He didn't say "Here are the ground rules," but I knew what he was doing when he said that everything must go back to the Scriptures. Our opinions about things were not so important as what the Scriptures would have to say about the subject at hand. Recalling that gave me some confidence that we would not end in disagreement. We would not have to agree to disagree. We would allow the Word of God to speak to the subject, and we would agree with His Word. That would settle the matter. I recalled how the Apostle Paul had instructed Timothy. He said that "All Scriptures is given by inspiration of God, and is profitable for doctrine, for reproof, for correction, for instruction in righteousness, that the man of God may be complete, thoroughly equipped for every good work" (2 Tim. 3:16-17). I always felt good when I could recall Scripture from memory. Scripture can be relied upon for instruction and that is what Solomon and I would do. Just as important is what the Apostle Peter had said about no prophecy of Scripture being a matter of any man's interpretation. Once again, that tells us that Scripture must interpret Scripture. Okay, now I felt better about bringing it up. As soon as Solomon came out of his study, I would ask him if we could talk.

When he did come out of his study, before I could open my mouth, he said, "You know, James, I could use some exercise. Why don't you and I walk down to the stream that you find so comforting and inspiring. We can talk along the way. How does that sound to you?"

"Sounds great to me," I said. "But on one condition."

"Oh, so now you are making conditions." he said. "What is your condition, James?"

"May I pick the subject for our conversation as we walk?" I asked.

"It sounds to me like there is something you want to get off your chest, my son."

"Yes, well, sort of, but at the same time I am seeking the truth and understanding about something."

"All right, James. My hope is that by the time we have returned you will feel wiser and less burdened."

We started walking towards the stream, and I began to tell him about my visit with my companions back at the settlement. I told him what the shepherd had to say the next morning concerning people being confused and concerned about what I had said the previous night. Then I told him that before I had left the camp, the issue of law had come up in my last discussion with one of the shepherds. I told him what the shepherd said about him wanting to bring Christians back under the law, but that Messiah had died to set us free from the law. By the time I had finished sharing these things with Solomon, we had reached the stream. It was only about a twenty-minute walk.

We arrived at the stream, and he said, "Where is it that you sit and pray, James?"

"I usually sit up against that old oak tree over there," I said.

"Then let's sit over there, shall we?" I nodded, and we walked over to the oak tree. "This is a nice place, James. I used to come here often myself. This stream runs down from the very top of the mountain. Did you know that, James?"

"No, I didn't, but I guessed that it did," I responded. I thought, did he even hear what I was telling him on the way here? Why wasn't he addressing that?

"It makes me think of the stream of life that flows out from under the temple in Ezekiel's vision. Are you aware of the vision that Ezekiel had concerning the temple?"

"Yes, one of the books I took from your study is about Ezekiel's vision. It's in my room, I just haven't had a chance to read it yet. However, one of the chapter headings concerns the stream."

"The stream is a river of life. It contains the Torah of God, the truth of God. The Apostle John saw the river flowing out from the very throne of God in his vision. Do you know why the truth of God is life, James?"

"I'm not sure what you are getting at," I said.

"Then listen more carefully and try to picture in your mind what I am saying to you. Make the important connection between what I just said to you about the river, the Word of God, and the truth and what I am about to say. Man does not live by bread alone but by every word that proceeds out of the mouth of God. When you sit by the stream, think on these things and allow the Holy Spirit to teach you. I bring this to your attention now, James, because of what you have shared with me on our way here. Once we are born again, the life within us flows from the very throne of God. I don't believe that anyone who is born again would dispute that. However, the life within us is also to flow out of us and be a source of life to others. The dispute lies there. Yeshua said to the Father, 'For I have given to them the words which You have given Me; and they have received them.' He also said of the Holy Spirit, 'However, when He, the Spirit of truth, has come, He will guide you into all truth; for He will not speak on His own authority, but whatever He hears He will speak.' You see, James, if we are speaking His words then we are allowing life to flow from us unto others. When we speak out of ourselves, out of our own souls, then we are not allowing His words to flow through us. This is especially important when we are speaking of the things of God, such as the law of God, the Torah. Sit down and let me speak to you concerning law. You determine for yourself if the words I speak are as the fresh waters of the stream.

"First of all, James, do you remember when we were discussing the word *Torah,* and I told you that *Torah* in English means 'instruction,' or 'hitting the mark'?"

"Yes, I remember. I said that it made a big difference to me to understand it as meaning 'instruction' rather than 'law.'"

"Yes, I recall you making that statement. We also discussed that the law was contained within the Torah, but the whole of Torah was not law. It is instruction. To walk in the instruction of God is necessary in order for that flow to continue from the throne to us and then from us to others. If we are not walking according to His instruction, we are walking in sin, because we are told in the Scriptures that sin is the breaking of the law. Whose law? God's law,

God's Torah. The word *walking* is a Hebrew idiom for *living Torah instruction.* That is why Scripture tells us that we are to walk as He walked."

I quickly commented, "You explained before that because we know He was a Torah observant Jew that means He walked in the Torah or His walk was in keeping the Torah, right?"

"Exactly!"

As Solomon continued instructing me in the Torah, I realized that there couldn't have been a better atmosphere than there by the stream. I could hear the water moving with his voice and feel a breeze gently blowing and the warm soft ground under me. I knew if this discussion was in his study, it somehow would not have been the same. I believed that Solomon knew this would be the ideal place to share some of these things that were challenging what I had believed all my life about being free from the law.

"The next important thing we had discussed," Solomon said, "was that Yeshua came to 'fulfill' the law, meaning that He came to fully explain the Torah of Moses, not to bring it to an end. In translating the Scriptures from Hebrew or Aramaic into the Greek and then from the Greek into English, the word *law* is used for eight different Greek words. There are also different kinds of law being referred to without a clear distinction unless one understands the context in which the word is being used. Sometimes *law* is a reference to Rabbinic law, which includes man-made law not from the Torah of

Moses. Rabbinic law is tradition established upon what is called the Oral Torah. The sages believe the Oral Torah was passed on from Moses to explain the written Torah. This is some of what Yeshua argued against with the Pharisees of His day. He did not want tradition taking the place of the Torah of Moses.

"Sometimes the Scripture is referring to covenant law and yet at other times to natural law. If the distinction is not made between law and instruction and between the different kinds of law, then confusion can reign. When confusion reigns, the devil takes advantage. However, the way to clear things up, is not to just classify the differences under one category of law, meaning the Torah, but to examine the Scripture and allow the original language of Scripture to clarify the distinctions. You see, James, it is not a simple matter, because the Torah is vital to our walk with God. The God that we serve intended the Torah to be a protection for His people. It is a kind of fence to keep us from wandering off into danger as well as to keep others from invading and destroying our home, so to speak. Most of the laws that govern society today on both sides of the mountain are taken from the Torah, such as laws against killing and stealing and bearing false witness and so on. Without these laws, if every man were left to govern himself and do what he thinks is right in his own eyes, we would have anarchy."

"May I ask you a question, Solomon?"

"Of course, James."

"Where did all of this 'freedom from the law' teaching that I have heard all my life, and that most everyone on my side of the mountain embraces, come from if not from the Scriptures?"

"That is a good question, James. You see, the Scriptures teach that our freedom is from the penalty of the law, which is what Messiah came to set us free from. The penalty of the law is death and death has been eradicated once we accept that Yeshua paid the penalty for our sins. Do you understand so far, James?"

"Yes, this makes perfect sense in light of what the gospel of salvation teaches us. But, why do we then teach that the whole law, including all the distinctions you mentioned, has been done away with?"

"There are many factors related to the full answer to that question. It has to do with misunderstanding the Scripture and a desire to separate from Israel and its ways and develop doctrines that were formed with a mixture of Scripture and philosophy. There was also the Christianizing of some of the pagan rituals brought in with people who embraced Christ as Lord and Savior but would not disregard the rituals and practices associated with their old pagan worship. Above all, the devil, as I said, has brought about confusion with half-truths and seductive ways just as he did in the garden with Eve. If he can keep apart those things that need to be brought together in order to fulfill the word of God, then he thinks he can defeat God's plan."

"What things have to be brought together?" I asked.

"For Christians, the Torah must be brought together with the belief in Yeshua as Messiah. For Jews, the belief in Yeshua as Messiah must be brought together with the Torah. It is then that Christianity and biblical Judaism can be united, thus uniting the two houses of Israel: the Northern Kingdom (Christianity) and the Southern Kingdom (the Jews). This will not be an easy task due to all the mixture of truth and falsehood through things added to the Scriptures on both sides of the mountain."

"I never saw that before. Things have to change on both sides of the mountain."

"Yes, James, and the Lord of the mountain is calling for the remnant to do just that today," he said. "It is all a part of His eternal plan. A plan that is laid out for us in the Scriptures."

Solomon continued, "The issue is further complicated when law is set against grace rather than finding grace in the law. Doing away with law in favor of grace appeals to the flesh but it is what some call 'cheap grace' and is not the design of God. He does not give grace instead of law. He gives us grace within the law, within the Torah. At the opening of John's gospel, we are told that the Torah was given through Moses, but grace and truth came through Yeshua. Many use this verse to justify the doctrine of no longer being under law. However, the Torah is full of grace and mercy. The greatest example of grace and mercy working together is in Yeshua's fulfilling of Passover, which is given in the Torah. He is the Passover Lamb who was slain for us. James, one cannot see the grace and truth within the Torah until we know how to rightly interpret it. That is why Yeshua came to fulfill the law, which means to rightly interpret the Torah, to fully explain the Torah to us. Also, the purpose of the Torah was never to give salvation, but to teach us how to live. Only the shed blood of Yeshua can justify someone and pay the penalty of their sins.

"They reject what they do not understand, James. This rejection is on both sides of the mountain. Remember, I rejected the truth that Yeshua is the Messiah of Israel until I was shown that He indeed fulfilled Scripture. I had to be willing to listen before I could hear. We must pray for the shepherds on both sides of the mountain to be willing to listen, James. We are told in the Scriptures that there is coming a judgment directed at the shepherds. We are also told of a stricter judgment for those who are teachers. We must pray for the shepherds, James.

"I feel so much better and I'm so much more hopeful for both sides of the mountain now, Solomon. Thank you for sharing these things with me."

Solomon decided to head back to the cabin, however, I remained at the stream for a time of contemplation and prayer. We had discussed a very important issue concerning the law, and I needed to let all of what Solomon had stated settle in. I knew that our next discussion was going to be an important one. It seemed to me that all of our discussions had led to the point where now I must act. We had talked the talk and now we must walk the walk. My hope was that our next discussion would provide me with an answer as to how. Then, I would pray for confirmation from the Lord. As the Scripture states by the witness of two or three a thing is established. This scriptural truth I had learned from Solomon. I would then need my direction established by that witness of two or three.

CHAPTER 17

The Puzzle

THE VERY NEXT DAY Solomon informed me, during breakfast, that his two friends were due to arrive around noon with more supplies. He was going to prepare a meal for them and discuss things on his side of the mountain. I found myself wishing I had someone from my side of the mountain who could bring me reports every so often, but that wasn't the case. After eating breakfast, I remained at the table while Solomon pulled things from the fridge and the pantry. The thought of someone coming from my side of the mountain with reports stayed with me and as Solomon continued speaking about the visitors, I kind of tuned him out and began, in my head, to count the days, or weeks, that I had been there. I remembered he had asked if I was willing to remain until we finished our conversation. With all we had left to discuss, it could take a lifetime, I thought. I then chuckled to myself and tuned Solomon back in.

I left Solomon to his preparations and headed out to the porch to read. Checking my watch, I noticed it was nearly noon and Solomon was still in the kitchen preparing the meal for his friends.

I went in and said, "Solomon, I'm going to let you visit with your friends and take a walk down to the stream."

He quickly responded, "You don't need to disappear, James. You are certainly welcome to eat with us and enjoy their company as well."

Still feeling a little awkward, like they would have to make conversation for me when they had so much to discuss among themselves, I said, "No, if you don't mind Solomon, I would like to spend some time with the LORD down by the stream."

"Okay then," he said, "I cannot compete with the LORD. Go and delight yourself in Him, and I will see you when you return."

I arrived at the stream, located my tree, and sat down. I began to pray through the things I so often prayed for: success for my companions in their pursuit of the high places; that the Holy Spirit would enter Solomon and my conversations; continued revelation concerning the joining of the two sides of the mountain at the top. I stopped and began to consider that part of the mission of Yeshua, the uniting of the two sides of the mountain: Judaism and Christianity. I thought about the gospel of the kingdom, which Solomon and I had talked about. I asked the LORD to please show me more about this gospel and how I was to walk before Him in light of it.

Propped up against the tree, with my eyes closed, my hands on the cool earth around me, my ears attuned to the sound of the stream, and my mind drifting towards the heavens, I waited there listening for His voice. As I sat in silence, my mind began to be filled with a vision. I saw what appeared to be hundreds of puzzle pieces laying in a pile. Then a pair of hands appeared and began to assemble the puzzle. The assembly began in the top left corner. As it progressed, I could see a deep dark color in that corner and, moving down a bit towards the middle, the pieces began to show a bright light extending outward. The hands then began to move down on the left side, filling in the border. The edge began to go from black to a mixture of greens and then as it continued down, there was some brown. The left edge of the puzzle was now finished from corner to corner.

The hands continued to take pieces from the pile and fill in from left to right. As the top was being filled in, I could see it was the cosmos. Pictured there were the sun, the moon, and the stars. Once the top was completed, the hands began to fill in downward towards the bottom. The earth came into view, as if seen from above. Then towards the bottom was pictured a place within the earth that I believe was the garden of Eden, because there was a man and a woman in a garden. The hands began to move across on the bottom. As piece after piece was added, I could see an ark floating on the water with a dove just above the ark. I was beginning to understand that these hands were forming the account of history given to us in the Bible, but why? I was completely mesmerized by what I was envisioning. I didn't dare move a muscle for fear that it would stop, so I sat still with my eyes closed watching this pair of hands continue to build this puzzle. There was no picking up a piece at a time and looking to see where the piece might fit. One hand simply scoped up a handful of pieces and then the other hand fit piece after piece exactly where each belonged. As I looked more closely I could see that the puzzle pieces in the pile had nothing on them. They were simply a grey color. I watched the specific picture on the piece appear as it was being put in place within the puzzle. God was creating the puzzle just as He created the things pictured within the puzzle.

My back was beginning to hurt a little from leaning up against the tree for so long, but I still did not dare to move in case the vision might end. As long as the vision went on, I would remain as still as possible. The puzzle was now being filled in from the bottom left. Just above the ark I could see what appeared to be an altar made of stone. Upon the altar was a young man bound and a man stood with a knife in his hand about to sacrifice the lad. Then the puzzle pieces completing the picture showed an angel holding the arm of who I realized was Abraham. Next, there appeared a parchment, and I could read only the word *covenant,* which was in English. The rest of the document was written in what must have been Hebrew. Just opposite the document was Abraham and with him were two younger men. A third picture appeared in the series running from the left and toward the middle. It was a picture of the two younger men. One was in an encampment in the desert with many tents and many people, while the other was standing in front of a pyramid. I understood this to represent Isaac and Jacob and their progeny.

I was now totally engulfed in the vision. It was as if I was moving through time as the events appeared, not even aware of my presence by the stream. Moving upwards towards the top border, the puzzle revealed the people of God enslaved in Egypt. Knowing what the Bible said of these events, I wanted to take the time to ponder each one, yet I could not because the hands continued working from the top and to the right and downward. The next thing that came into view was Moses coming down from Mt. Sinai with the tablets. Then just below that came a spectacularly bright light, as if shining with the brilliance of polished gold, bursting forth from the tabernacle of Moses. All of the puzzle that had been filled in from the corner darkness outward was beautiful in color and detail, however, this brilliant light made all that came before it seem dull in comparison. I couldn't imagine anything more glorious in appearance.

The hands now picked up speed and moved quickly through the anointing of Saul as the first king of Israel to

David slaying Goliath and then to the anointing of this man who would become beloved by Israel and by God Himself. During the time when I lived on my side of the mountain, I had a picture on the wall of one of my dwelling places. It was a picture of the major prophets of Israel: Isaiah, Jeremiah, and Ezekiel. That exact picture was now laid out by the hands filling in the puzzle, showing the time of the prophets. The hands were almost to the middle of the puzzle as the hands quickly finished the border all around allowing me to determine that the midpoint of the puzzle had been reached. After the picture of the prophets, the puzzle portrayed the death of King Solomon and the separation of Israel into the Northern and Southern Kingdoms. Once again, I saw a sequence of three pictures moving from the center down to the bottom. The first of the three pictures illustrated the defeat of the Northern Kingdom and its people disbursed into the nations of the world. I saw them bound to each other and being led away. The second picture within this sequence was the defeat of the Southern Kingdom. Here was pictured the temple burning and the people bound to each other and being lead to Babylon. In the third picture of the sequence was Daniel the prophet kneeling on a balcony, humbly bowed in prayer with the light of heaven shining down upon him.

As the hands continued filling in and moving from the bottom of the frame all the way to the top, I was suddenly unable to see anything clearly. It was as if events were actually there, but a kind of fog or mist lay over each picture from the bottom to the top making it so I could not figure out what lay underneath. Then, as the hands filled in another section from top to bottom, it again became bright and clear. A brightness like in the picture of the tabernacle of Moses filled a large section of the puzzle. Once it was finished, from top to bottom, there was the picture of the Messiah being baptized and a dove descending from heaven. The cross of Messiah was superimposed over the bright light of the dove, and beside the cross in the light was the Messiah standing by the open grave that had held Him. This was by far the brightest portion within the entire puzzle to that point. It also occupied more space than anything else previously pictured.

The hands continued to fill in the rest of the puzzle, but right then I could not take my eyes away from the brilliance of the last picture. When I finally looked past this picture, I saw that the hands were forming pictures within the puzzle depicting the history of Israel and its suffering as the Southern Kingdom was once again dispersed by the Romans into the nations. I saw the Holocaust as piles of naked bodies thrown on top of one another by German soldiers. Then I saw the Israeli flag flying, and I knew it was at the time when Israel had come home to their land and to Jerusalem. This section was laid out mostly from the center down to the bottom of the puzzle.

The hands then began working from the middle upward to the border. I could see it was filling in the history of Christianity. Portrayed here was the Vatican in Rome and a glorious cathedral, which I recognized as existing to this day in England. There were also large tent meetings occurring in many places throughout the land.

I thought this would complete the puzzle but there was still some room left after these pictures to the right edge of the puzzle. Also, there were still puzzle pieces left in the pile. I then saw one hand move over to the pile of grey puzzle pieces still left, causing them to shine brilliantly. All I could see on those pieces was an unconstrained light. Both hands then scooped up these pieces and simply dropped them into the remaining space of the puzzle. Immediately they all fit in perfectly, forming simply an area of splendid light. Then two words began to form within this light. These two words came through in crimson red: *Millennial Reign*.

I thought certainly at this point the vision would end, but it did not. The hands were no longer in view, but the puzzle lay there. I just looked at the whole thing and studied it for a time. Then the hands returned and began doing something that shocked me. As if ripping the puzzle apart, the hands removed a section, the brightest section showing the Messiah's baptism and His cross with Him standing between the cross and the empty grave. Taking this section, the hands laid it beside the puzzle. Then both things came into view, the puzzle with that gaping hole and the section that had been removed sitting beside the puzzle. I watched but couldn't grasp its full meaning. A moment passed before anything else happened. Then, above the puzzle was written the name Israel. Above the piece removed was written Christianity.

I cried out, "Lord, please tell me what this means!"

Then came the voice of the Lord. "Israel is My chosen people, and there can be no salvation outside of the covenant that I have with Israel. My covenant can only be fulfilled through the Messiah, Yeshua. Israel rejected their Messiah, and so He is removed from Israel. Christianity received the Messiah, but it has divorced itself from Israel and must come to acknowledge that through faith in Messiah, they are grafted into Israel. The puzzle must be completed and restoration must be accomplished. These things must happen on both sides of the mountain. Israel must accept the Messiah. Christianity must acknowledge that it is only through Israel and the covenant with Abraham and his offspring that salvation comes to mankind. It is through understanding and embracing the oracles and commandments that all My people will know the full restoration and blessing of the God of Israel."

The puzzle was finished and the vision ended. The Lord had faithfully spoken to me, giving me some understanding. I began to weep. I was not weeping from sadness nor from joy. I didn't really know why I was weeping. Perhaps it was because I felt so honored that the Lord would allow me to see such a glorious and moving vision. I stood to my feet and my body pained. I think it had stayed tensed throughout the vision, and I needed to stretch. So, I began to stretch and walk from the tree to the stream to refresh myself. I cupped my hands, took some water, and splashed it onto my face. It felt wonderful, so I did it a few more times. I then decided it was time to head back to the cabin. What would I tell Solomon? What would he think? What do I think?

CHAPTER 18

The Elijah Task:
History Speaking

WHILE WALKING BACK TO the cabin, my mind kept going from the conversation with Solomon the day before about Christianity and Judaism to the vivid vision I just had. It seemed like the Holy Spirit was trying to weave the two together. Then it struck me. After the vision I had fervently prayed for understanding. Was the Holy Spirit now trying to tell me the vision was somehow tied to what I needed to know concerning my role on my side of the mountain?

I prayed, "Lord, please also give Solomon some understanding of this vision and how it may be linked to what you want me to do."

I arrived back at the cabin around the middle of the afternoon and found Solomon sweeping the front porch. He heard me approach, looked up, smiled, and then continued sweeping. I walked up the steps and nodded as I continued past him and into the cabin. Needing to lie down and rest before dinner, I went to my room, laid down on my bed, and quickly fell asleep. I slept for about two hours. When I awoke, I simply laid in bed, staring up at the ceiling and thinking about how to share the vision with Solomon. It didn't take long before I decided I'd first write down the vision and give it to him to read. Then, if he was willing, we could discuss it in light of our conversation just before I received the vision. Rising from my bed, I went to the desk in my room and began writing. The words just flowed out of me, and I felt like I was experiencing it all over again. Several times I had to halt my writing just to thank the Lord and ponder the intent of the vision. While I wasn't sure what I had been shown, I had no doubt that it came from my Lord. A thought entered my mind: if the Lord was going to give a vision, why wouldn't He just tell me what it meant? Why the need to search out the meaning? That would be another good question for Solomon. Solomon was appropriately named. He certainly had much wisdom, and it was obviously not just given to him in a flash. He had studied the ways of the Lord all his life.

When I went downstairs to give the written vision to Solomon, I couldn't find him anywhere. That's odd, I thought. He always tells me if he's going somewhere. I went to his office to look out the windows to see if he was out back, but I still couldn't see him. Just then, I heard something in the shed, so I put the papers on his desk and ran out back to see if he was in the shed and was all right. Sure enough, Solomon was in the shed sharpening the two axes.

"It's interesting to see you out here sharpening the axes, Solomon. I'm saying that because I need a sharp mind to help me with something."

"What is it that you need help with, James?"

"Well, after you left the stream, I received a very detailed vision from the Lord, but I am not sure I understand its meaning."

"You have not given yourself much time to consider it, James. Perhaps you ought to spend some time in prayer and allow the Lord to share its meaning with you."

"Yes, I intend to do that Solomon, but I'm so excited about it, I wrote it down for you to read so that together we might both consider it before the Lord. You know the old saying, 'Two heads are better than one.'" Solomon looked up from sharpening the ax and gave me one of those "Really?" looks. As he continued to sharpen the ax, he said, "I will read your vision. However, I want you, to tell me what you hear from the Lord about the vision. Then I will add, if need be, what I believe I have heard from the Lord. Where did you put the vision you have for me to consider?"

"It's on your desk in your study. Will you read it soon?"

"Yes, James. I will read it during my evening prayer time."

"When will we be able to discuss it?"

"That depends upon when the Lord decides to disclose to you its meaning. You should now go and get the table set for dinner. I will be along in a few moments to get cleaned up and begin the meal."

With the vision still heavy on my mind, I went inside and set the table and then sat on the porch, closed my eyes, and began to think about the vision, allowing it to flow into my mind once more as I asked the Lord to speak to me. I replayed the vision over and over again and knew it was an unfolding of biblical history. The thing that struck me the most was the word Israel over the puzzle with the hole in it, where the hands had removed the time of Messiah and the word *Christianity* above the section that was removed and laid beside the puzzle. I kept looking at these two distinct sections and all of a sudden, the words *Elijah Task* came to my mind. Elijah Task? What was that supposed to mean? I had no idea what these words had to do with the puzzle, but I was pretty sure the Lord was speaking to me. I started to think about Elijah. I knew he was a prophet. I remembered that he had been taken to heaven in a fiery chariot, but I couldn't remember exactly what he prophesied. Okay, I thought. At least I have some place to start. I'll go upstairs and get my Bible and read about Elijah. Maybe some of this will start to make sense.

Going inside, I headed toward the stairs. As I passed Solomon in the kitchen, I paused slightly and said, "I think I got something from the Lord, Solomon."

There was no response from him, but I knew he had heard me. Arriving at my bedroom, I went inside and grabbed my Bible from off the dresser and sat in the chair by the window. I found that the history of Elijah was recorded in 1 Kings, so I began at chapter one in order to try and get the whole picture. After about an hour, I heard Solomon call me for dinner. I closed my Bible, washed up, and headed downstairs. Anxious to tell Solomon about the words *Elijah Task*, when I arrived at the table I began to speak.

Solomon put his hand up to quiet me and said, "Let's thank the Lord. Why don't you begin by giving Him thanks for all that has taken place today, at the stream and up in your room and, of course, for His provision of which we are about to partake."

I calmed myself down, took a deep breath, and began to pray. When I was finished, Solomon followed with an amen and we sat to eat. I wasn't sure if I should speak or not, so I just began to eat as did Solomon. Finally, he broke the silence. "So, you believe that you have heard from the Lord about your vision?"

"Yes," was all I responded. A few bites later, I continued by asking Solomon if he had read the vision yet.

He said, "No, James. I didn't want to rush through reading it. I will read it during my prayer time tonight, when I can thoughtfully consider it."

"I'm sorry that I am so anxious about this, but it is the most unusual vision I have ever received from the Lord. I can't get it off my mind."

"Allow me to read it tonight and then we can begin to discuss it after prayer. Many times, as you know, the Lord reveals things through a conversation. Let's plan for around eight o'clock, shall we? You may also share with me what you believe the Lord had spoken to you out on the porch."

His words set well with me, and I actually breathed a sigh of relief causing Solomon to chuckle a bit. After dinner, I began cleaning off the table and putting the leftovers away as Solomon headed for his study to begin his evening prayers. I knew that he was in there reading the vision because I could hear the papers rustle as he would go from one page to another. I couldn't help but wonder what he was thinking. While drying the dishes, I found myself picking up a dish, begin wiping it, and moving toward his slightly opened study door. Then I would return to the sink, put down the dried dish, and grab another one and follow the same routine.

When I had finished cleaning up, I knew I should return to the Bible and my reading on Elijah, but I was just too anxious. So I headed back out onto the porch. The night air was cool and refreshing, and I could hear the wind blowing in the trees. God's act of creation entered my mind. The sun had set, and the sky was just dark enough so that you could begin to see the stars. I sat on the steps and began to thank the Lord for His creation. Inside the cabin I was all wound up, but sitting under the night sky in the cool evening air and listening to the sound of the rustling trees calmed me.

I said to the Lord, "All of this You have created for us. Your creation and the sense of your presence and your love brings peace. Thank you, Lord, for who You are and for Your great love toward us." Even though I was more relaxed, I still kept looking at my watch waiting for eight o'clock to come. Finally, I went inside and right to Solomon's study.

Even before I reached the door Solomon said, "Come in, James." I entered the room and he motioned for me to sit. I sat and realized I had this big grin on my face, like some little child knowing he was about to receive some kind of reward. I then felt very awkward. Solomon just sat there looking at me not saying a word, and I sat there waiting for him to speak. Finally, he said, "Very interesting vision, James. What do you believe the Lord spoke to you today concerning it?"

"Well, while I was out on the porch running the vision through my mind again, the Lord had me focus on the two separate things: one, the puzzle without the scene of Messiah and the word *Israel* above it and two, the picture of Messiah outside the puzzle with the word *Christianity* over it. Then I heard the words *Elijah Task.*"

"Elijah Task," he repeated. "That's interesting. Are you able to make any connection, James?"

"No, not yet. I went upstairs and began to read the account of Elijah, but I haven't finished it yet. So no, I can't make any connection."

"Well, James, I believe this vision is certainly from the Lord, and I believe that He would have us understand it. Therefore, let me propose what we should do. In light of the term *Elijah Task,* that you heard while seeking to understand the vision before the Lord, let's begin to do an in-depth study of Elijah and his ministry. Let's both prayerfully read the Scriptures concerning Elijah and come together each day to discuss what we have learned and what we believe the Lord to have revealed to increase or enlighten our learning."

"So, you don't have any understanding of what the vision is about?" I asked.

"I have some thoughts about it, James. However, I would like to take some time to consider those thoughts, especially now in light of the Elijah Task. I know we both have that looming question, 'What is the Elijah Task?' Let's begin with trying to find an answer to that question. We can first look at the historical biblical account of what Elijah was commissioned to do, and with some certainty speak of what the Elijah Task was according to that account. We can then look at the words of Yeshua concerning John the Baptist coming in the spirit and power of Elijah, and from the account of John's proclamation determine what is meant by Yeshua's statement concerning John."

"Oh, yes. I forgot about Yeshua referring to John the Baptist as Elijah. We can compare what Elijah was sent by God to proclaim and determine if what John was sent to proclaim had any similarity. Then we would have the witness of two of which you speak so often."

"Yes, James. Through a search of these two historical and biblical accounts we can determine with some certainty what the Elijah Task entailed, for both Elijah the prophet and John the Baptist."

"One thing comes to mind as we are speaking, Solomon. In light of what we just said, the Elijah Task must be prophetic, and, if the Lord is speaking that to me, the puzzle must have a prophetic message to it."

"That would seem to be the case, James, but let's not jump ahead too quickly. We need to study, to show ourselves approved to God, and allow the Holy Spirit to instruct us through our study and our conversations."

"I know," I said. "I need to calm down and trust the Lord to reveal these things in His time. Another thing, I don't think the Bible ever uses the term *Elijah Task*, does it?"

"I don't believe so, James." However, if it was the Lord who spoke it to you, there is significance in His using it. Though the Bible doesn't use the term, both men were commissioned by the God of Israel to complete a calling, a task, given to them for the people of their generations."

"Do you think the Lord could be speaking to us about a calling of God, in this hour, for this generation, having similarities to the callings upon Elijah the prophet and John the Baptist?"

"We can only pray that the Lord would make it clear to us, James. In order to take on such a profound task, we would need to be certain within ourselves that it is truly the calling of God. Otherwise, we could certainly be turned back at the first sign of resistance. You are aware of the resistance that both these men faced as they went forth in the power and anointing of God, aren't you? Elijah was found hiding in a cave at one point."

"I know. One step at a time, right Solomon?"

"Yes, James. Like putting a puzzle together. I will say good night now, James. I am very excited by what you have brought into my home. By the grace of God, we shall move forward with it."

"Good night, Solomon," I said as I departed from the study. I prayed that the Lord would give me a dream that night bringing further understanding and insight concerning the vision.

That night I did have a dream in the night, but I did not believe it was from the Lord. I think the dream had more to do with my anxiety. It was a very frustrating dream full of ridiculous situations. It made no sense at all. As I awoke and got ready for the day I pondered my dream and thought this one was definitely not of God. It was to be a day of study and prayer. I thought about returning to the stream, but then I decided my time would be better served tucked away in my room, taking in all I could from the Scriptures concerning Elijah and John the Baptist. As soon as I heard Solomon moving around, I went to meet him in the hallway on his way downstairs. I told him I had decided to fast and that I would not be down for breakfast, lunch, or dinner. He told me he thought it was a good idea and asked if I wanted to meet in the evening around the same time as last night. I said I would very much like to do that, and we parted ways for the day. I don't know what Solomon did because I didn't leave my room the entire day. There was a glass in the bathroom adjoining my bedroom, so I had plenty of water to drink during the day and I didn't need to go down to the kitchen.

I continued to explore the biblical account of Elijah. I learned that just prior to his death, King Solomon had appointed Jeroboam, one of his servants from the tribe of Ephraim, to oversee the needs of the house of Joseph, which were composed of the tribes of Ephraim and Manasseh, Joseph's two sons. This individual Jeroboam played a major role in the formation of what came to be known as the two houses or kingdoms of Israel.

After Solomon's death, his son Rehoboam reigned in his place. The people refused to follow him, except for the tribes of Judah and Benjamin. The other ten tribes of Israel were eventually ruled by Jeroboam. Thus, two kingdoms of Israel came into being. Those under the rule of Solomon's son Rehoboam were called the Southern Kingdom because they dwelt in the southern region. Those under the rule of Jeroboam were called the Northern Kingdom.

I found that there were many kings who reigned and many prophets who served between the time of Jeroboam and King Ahab, the history of which is recorded in 1 Kings. There was one particular king and one particular prophet I thought with whom Solomon and I should be mainly concerned: King Ahab and the prophet Elijah. I read the following concerning King Ahab: "Now Ahab the son of Omri did evil in the sight of the LORD, more than all who were before him" (1 Kings 16:30). I then read how King Ahab angered the LORD:

> And it came to pass, as though it had been a trivial thing for him to walk in the sins of Jeroboam the son of Nebat, that he took as wife Jezebel the daughter of Ethbaal, king of the Sidonians; and he went and served Baal and worshiped him. Then he set up an altar for Baal in the temple of Baal, which he had built in Samaria. And Ahab made a wooden image. Ahab did more to provoke the LORD God of Israel to anger than all the kings of Israel who were before him. (1 Kings 16:31-33)

I thought about all of the rebellious deeds that were going on and began to understand how the Lord would have reason to become so angry. It's a wonder He didn't just destroy them all, and yet He always seemed to desire to provide a way of return for them. He is truly a God of new beginnings, I thought, and that was something I needed to remember, in light of the vision and possibly the new task associated with it.

I returned to my reading and found that Elijah the prophet of God went into hiding because Queen Jezebel was having all the prophets of God killed. When I read this, I thought, how would she ever dare to do such a thing? Then I realized she thought her gods were greater than the God of Israel. Hmm, I thought again, how did these people come up with all these false gods? A good question for Solomon. He seemed to know so much about ancient history I was sure he'd have an answer. Then I realized I was being drawn off subject, and I returned to my study of Elijah.

The Northern Kingdom was suffering a drought because the Lord had Elijah prophesy that no rain would fall on them due to the sins of the people (see 1 Kings 17). The Lord then called Elijah out of hiding and sent him to prophesy judgment. This judgment at Mount Carmel is recorded in chapter 18 and was a rebuke of the king and the people for engaging in "mixed worship."

The Scripture didn't use the term *mixed worship*, but when I read what was going on, it was as if the Lord just interjected into my mind that phrase. I quickly made a note of this thought and re-read the judgment at Mount Carmel. "And Elijah came to all the people, and said, 'How long will you falter between two opinions? If the Lord is God, follow Him; but if Baal, follow him" (1 Kings 18:21). It became obvious to me that the people had entered into a form of mixed worship by worshiping both the God of Israel and Baal. Otherwise, why would Elijah say what he had said to them? How easily we can be led astray even after God teaches us all we need to know in order to worship Him in spirit and in truth. How attracted we are to all those religious traditions and forms of worship that are so contrary to the ways of the God of Israel.

The kind of worship that the God of Israel desires was laid out for them at Mount Sinai. Moses was on the mountain for forty days learning the ways of the Lord so that he could teach the people. Being slaves in Egypt in the midst of all kinds of idol worship for so long, and not free to worship their God, they needed to be taught how He was to be worshiped.

The people who had entered into covenant with the God of Israel at Mount Sinai were once again breaking that covenant. The Lord sent Elijah to warn them and to give them an opportunity to repent and return to the true worship of the God of Israel as instructed by Moses. I had to stop and reflect on this loving Father who wanted to be one with His people. Yes, this was about judgment, but it was about love as well. Truly, He was judging them in order to call them back to be with Him and to know His blessings for their lives.

I sat there for a moment considering judgment. I remembered how, during my ascent up the mountain, when I had turned away from God, He had sent his fire to drive me back to the stream where I could once again hear His voice and know His love. I had referred to that judgment as the fire of His love. It was good to recall that experience in light of what I was now reading. It was good to remember that God often judges His people to drive us back to Him, back to the place of blessing, because He so loves us.

The task of Elijah was becoming clearer to me. Elijah was to deliver the Word of the Lord concerning this mixed worship and to redirect the people to the true and pure worship of the Lord. He was calling for repentance so that once again the people could know the favor of the Lord. So that, once again, the rains would come and water the land producing the crops needed to feed the people. So that, once again, the rain of the Holy Spirit could fall upon the people.

The day was only half over, and I felt filled with a knowledge I had not known before. I closed my Bible and took notes of all I had learned and then I began to pray. I asked the Lord to simplify all this information so that Solomon and I could have a meaningful conversation that evening. I lay down on the bed and continued to pray. When I awoke, I looked at my watch and realized that I had slept for over an hour. I quickly got up and grabbed my Bible and notes. Taking them to the chair by the window, I began to quickly scan the notes and then returned to the Scriptures to continue my study.

I opened my Bible to the book of Malachi. I was about to turn to 1 Kings when I noticed the name Elijah in the print before me. I read the following:

> Behold, I will send you Elijah the prophet before the coming of the great and dreadful day of the LORD. And he will turn the hearts of the fathers to the children, and the hearts of the children to their fathers, lest I come and strike the earth with a curse. (Malachi 4:5-6)

I was sure the Spirt of God must have led me to that particular passage. I turned to the commentary on those verses in my Bible, and it said that this passage was about the second coming of the Lord.

I rested my Bible on my lap, looked out the window, and asked the Lord what He was trying to show me. In this passage we are told that Elijah is coming again for a specific purpose. He is to turn the hearts of the fathers to their children. I stopped there and remembered that Solomon often spoke of the fathers as being Abraham, Isaac, and Jacob—in other words Israel. He is coming again to turn the hearts of Israel to the children. Who were the children? I reasoned that the children may be those who had come in through the preaching of the gospel of salvation, in other words, the church. He is to turn the hearts of the fathers (Israel) to the children (the church) and the hearts of the children (the church) to their fathers (Abraham, Isaac, and Jacob, or Israel). All this made perfect sense to me. Much of what Solomon and I had discussed during my time with him was the uniting of the two sides of the mountain: Judaism and Christianity. I began to get really excited. Things were coming together. I wasn't sure if my interpretation was biblical, but I knew because Solomon and I studied the Scriptures, the Bible would clarify things for us, especially if this was all from God.

As I sat back in my chair, I noticed it was beginning to rain. My window was open, and the wind began to pick up along with the rain. The dirt pathway in the valley turned darker as the rain settled into it. Once again, I was reminded of my former life. There I was in my little house on the beach. The house where I received my calling to begin my ascent up the mountain. I remembered thinking of all the people resting and playing on the beach and how, when a sudden storm would come, they would all scurry to their cars and homes. I recalled watching how the rain would change the color of the sand on the beach and eventually erase all evidence that anyone had ever been there. I could have sat there and mused over those memories, but a sudden wet wind blew in through the window and startled me back to my task.

My finger was still holding my place in the Bible. I opened once again to Malachi and re-read the passage. I then thought about this new Elijah who was to come again, what he would speak and do. Elijah was a prophet, one who speaks for God, the very words of God. Therefore, I thought, the way in which this coming Elijah is going to accomplish his task would be through a prophetic calling and a prophetic pronouncement. Once again, I recalled a time during my ascent when the Lord of the mountain told me that the church was to have a prophetic voice. Well, I reasoned, if the church is to have a prophetic voice, then so must Judaism. Two prophetic voices on the mountain of the Lord calling out to those ascending the mountain on both sides. Two witnesses to what God is saying to this generation.

What words will this coming Elijah be speaking? Will he be given the same prophetic task as the first Elijah? Then I thought of John the Baptist. If Yeshua referred to him as being Elijah, did he have the same task? What did he speak to the people of his day? I looked down at my Bible once again. "Remember the Law of Moses, My servant, which I commanded him in Horeb for all Israel, with the statutes and judgments. Behold, I will send you Elijah the prophet before the coming of the great and dreadful day of the LORD" (Malachi 4:4-5). Isn't that what John the Baptist did? Didn't he rebuke the elders of Israel the same way that Elijah rebuked the King of Israel? Wasn't it for the same cause of adding to the Law of Moses? In Ahab's day, it was a false god added to the worship of the God of Israel. In John's day it was about adding to the Torah those things that were heavy burdens for the people to bear, that were not a part of the Torah of Moses. Both created a form of mixed worship. I recalled the issue of doctrines within the church that Solomon and I had discussed earlier and that too would enter in here. I had to study more about John.

CHAPTER 19

The Spirit
and the Power of Elijah

EVENING HAD FINALLY COME, and it was time to meet with Solomon. As I went down stairs and smelled the dinner that Solomon had enjoyed, I felt very hungry. However, I didn't regret fasting at all and felt the day had produced some incredible results. I looked forward to sharing everything with Solomon. True to his word, as always, Solomon was in his study awaiting my arrival.

"I see you are carrying some notes, James." Solomon said, as I walked in.

"Yes, Solomon, I have a great deal to share. I would like to begin with prayer, though, if you don't mind."

"Of course, I don't mind, James. We both know we cannot advance in spiritual matters without the help of the Lord. After all it was He who said that the reason He would send the Holy Spirit was to lead us into all truth."

That needed no response. I simply sat in the chair opposite Solomon, and after praying we were ready to begin.

Solomon immediately opened the session. "I would like to begin with a couple of passages. Let's read them together. The first is Matthew 17:11-13:

> Jesus answered and said to them, "Indeed, Elijah is coming first and will restore all things. But I say to you that Elijah has come already, and they did not know him but did to him whatever they wished. Likewise, the Son of Man is also about to suffer at their hands." Then the disciples understood that He spoke to them of John the Baptist.

"The second passage is Luke 1:13-17:

> But the angel said to him, "Do not be afraid, Zachariah, for your prayer is heard; and your wife Elizabeth will bear you a son, and you shall call his name John. And you will have joy and gladness, and many will rejoice at his birth. For he will be great in the sight of the Lord, and shall drink neither wine nor strong drink. He will also be filled with the Holy Spirit, even from his mother's womb. And he will turn many of the children of Israel to the Lord their God. He will also go before Him in the spirit and power of Elijah, to turn the hearts of the fathers

to the children, and the disobedient to the wisdom of the just, to make ready a people prepared for the Lord."

"Now we are considering three things here, James. First, we are determining Elijah's Task, by a study of biblical history. Second, we are trying to determine if John the Baptist played the same role or had the same task in Yeshua's day. And third, we are looking to understand the task of the coming Elijah during the day of the Lord."

"I have a question, Solomon. When the Scripture speaks of the day of the Lord, I believe I recall you teaching me that it is not speaking of a single twenty-four-hour day, but it is speaking of the thousand-year reign of Yeshua as the seventh day. Is that correct?"

"Yes, James, that's correct. And if you recall, the day begins with the evening, which in this seventh day, is the darkness, and the darkness speaks of the tribulation period."

"So, will this second coming of Elijah be during the tribulation period?"

"Yes, and if the vision the Lord gave you is connected to the Elijah Task of these last days, then it will most likely occur during the day of the Lord. Or it could be during a time just prior to the day of the Lord in preparation for that day. A great deal of this is our speculation so we must be disciplined to examine everything we suppose against

Scripture. We must allow anything that is contrary to the Word of God fall away.

We talked for more than two hours and then ended with prayer before retiring to our rooms. When I got to my room, I laid out all my notes on the bed to put them in order. I had taken notes so quickly that many things were underlined or highlighted with an asterisk or circled, and I needed to organize them. I would've preferred to wait until morning, but I knew I had a great deal more studying to do the next day for I had to try and keep up with Solomon.

After an hour of sorting and organizing, I decided to read through everything in order, and then turn in for the night.

We are told that John will be directed by the Holy Spirit to speak the words of God and that as he does, those words will turn many of the children of Israel to the Lord their God.

Q) Turn them from what?
A) Turn them from a form of mixed worship. He will do this in the spirit and power of Elijah! That is exactly what the prophet Malachi prophesied would happen.

Q) Did John do that?
A) John's message was a message of repentance. He

was calling the people to return to the true worship of God. Like Elijah before him, he addressed the mixed worship of his day.

Q) To what end?
A) To prepare the way of the Lord.

Q) What is the way of the Lord?
A) Yeshua came to fulfill, to live the Torah of God, the way of the Lord. He offered pure and perfect living and worship to the Father as an example for us.

Scripture: 1 John 2:6: "He who says he abides in Him ought himself also to walk just as he walked."
Note: Your walk is a Hebrew idiom, meaning the way you live your life.

Conclusion: The Pharisees had added so many man-made traditions to the Torah that they had violated it to the point that they were once again walking out a form of mixed worship. It was a mixture of the Word of God with the traditions and doctrines of man, where one absolutely violates the other.

Note: Yeshua addressed the Pharisees over and over again concerning this issue. These encounters are recorded for us in the gospels. Example: Matthew 23:4-5, 13, "For they bind heavy burdens, hard to

bear, and lay them on men's shoulders; but they
themselves will not move them with one of their
fingers. But all their works they do to be seen by men.
. . . But woe to you, scribes and Pharisees, hypocrites!
For you shut up the kingdom of heaven against men."
Conclusion: Yeshua came to live biblical Judaism
as an example for us and not rabbinic Judaism with
all its man-made traditions. He came to fulfill the
law/Torah and the prophets, meaning to fully live in
God's truth found in the Word of God, the Torah
and the prophets.

Scripture: Matthew 5:17-18

Q) Now, if that was the case during the days of Elijah
and was also the case during the days of John the
Baptist, who came in the spirit and power of Elijah,
what about today? Is there mixed worship in the
church on my side of the mountain? Is there mixed
worship within Judaism on Solomon's side of the
mountain?
A) There is much confusion on my side of the
mountain within the church and a tremendous
amount of disagreement as to how God ought to be
worshiped and faith in Him walked out. Solomon
asserts the same for his side of the mountain.
Conclusion: Many within the church today believe
we are that last generation who will see the second

coming of the Lord. According to Solomon, many within Judaism believe the Messiah of Israel is coming soon, in this generation. On my side of the mountain we sing a song titled "These are the days of Elijah."

Q.) Are they? If so, what does that truly mean for us?

CHAPTER 20

The Restoration

WHEN I WOKE THE next morning still feeling very tired, I asked the Lord if I should fast again. I entered a time of prayer while lying there in my bed. Not having heard, or perhaps not wanting to hear the Lord on the subject of fasting, I reasoned it would be counterproductive to fast because I would be too tired to study effectively.

I couldn't smell breakfast cooking and I said to myself, "Please Lord, don't let Solomon choose to fast today." I knew I was being selfish, but I was really hungry. I got dressed and went downstairs to see what was going on. Solomon didn't cook anything for breakfast. He decided instead we would have fruit and juice for breakfast that morning. It was not what I had hoped for, but it was very tasty, and I somewhat enjoyed it. I didn't hesitate to ask him what he had planned for lunch though. He gave me another one of those "raised eyebrow" looks, what I call the "really" look. I couldn't put anything over on him. He knew I was not really pleased with the breakfast and was hoping for a substantial lunch.

"I thought it would be good for you, even coming off just a one-day fast to eat lightly," Solomon said.

After the meager breakfast I went upstairs to wash up and get ready to begin studying, when it occurred to me that I didn't ask Solomon about what we should study today. I ran back downstairs and found him cleaning up after breakfast. I quickly said, "Solomon, I'm so sorry. I'm supposed to be doing that. I am just so engrossed in this study I completely forgot to clean up. Please let me do it."

"I don't ever want you to feel compelled to serve, James. I want you to serve only from a willing heart."

"I assure you it is from a willing heart that I serve here." I took the cloth from his hand and began to wash the dishes. As he headed for the living room, I called out to him and asked if there was anything in particular that we should study today.

He responded, "I don't expect you to keep track of these things, James, but today is the day my two friends will be bringing up supplies. Let's allow the Lord to direct us as to what He would have us study today. I suggest you wait on Him and not push ahead until He, who is faithful, leads you."

"Well, is there anything you would like me to do while I am waiting on the Lord, Solomon?"

"Yes, James. I would like you to visit with me and my friends today. I want them to get to know you and for you to get to know them. There may be a time when the Lord leads you to go to the other side of the mountain and it would be good for you to know them. Perhaps they could help you while you are there."

"Alright, Solomon. I'll gladly visit with them."

I went back upstairs to await his friends' arrival. Instead of opening the Bible, I returned to the book on Zion that I had taken from Solomon's study. I began to read about the restoration of the temple that Ezra undertook after Israel's time in Babylon. The temple had been destroyed and needed to be restored so that those coming out of captivity could resume the temple service. I found the account to be very interesting. There was a little more history in the book than the Bible actually provided. The thing that stood out to me the most was the issue of restoration. To restore something is to bring it back to its original condition. Once again, I thought of the puzzle. What was it going to take to restore the puzzle back to its original condition? What would it take to place the removed scene back into the puzzle?

I didn't realize it, but I had been reading for well over two hours when I heard voices coming from outside. I reckoned it was Solomon's visitors, so I set the book down and went downstairs. It appeared they were going to visit outside on the porch. Solomon had not made them lunch as he usually did.

When I stepped onto the porch, Solomon quickly said, "Ah, here is James. Come, sit with us, James."

Solomon had brought out the kitchen chairs so that we could all sit and visit.

I extended my hand to them, but instead of shaking my hand they both tipped their hat to me and said, "It is good to see you again, James. We are looking forward to our conversation."

They began to ask me many questions about my stay with Solomon and to let me know how much I should appreciate his hospitality. I told them I would rather be no place else and that I was learning so much from him. I also told them he was like a father to me. Solomon smiled and thanked me for that remark.

I expected a discussion about what was happening on their side of the mountain. The discussion stayed on me for a while as they continued to ask me how I came to be there and what my life was like on my side of the mountain. Then finally, Solomon asked if they would tell me what it was like living on their side of the mountain. The older of the two began. "There are many things that must be restored on our side of the mountain," he said. Ah, I thought, there You are Lord. There is my second witness. You want me to focus on restoration now in my studies. The rest of what they said kind of just went in one ear and out the other, as the saying goes because, from that moment on, I just wanted to get back upstairs and do a search on restoration throughout Scripture. However, we enjoyed one another's company for a time and then they departed extending me a welcome to come and visit them

any time I was on their side of the mountain. I thanked
them and said good-by as they departed.

As I helped Solomon return the chairs to the kitchen,
I shared with him how the issue of restoration had come
up twice that morning. He said, "Well then, James, let us
study the issue of restoration and come together tonight
with our findings. You remember we have already touched
on the issue in our study. Yeshua said, 'Elijah is coming
first and will restore all things.' He was not speaking about
John the Baptist who had already come. He was speaking
about a future event. He was speaking about His second
coming."

I started my study with the Scripture that Solomon
had just mentioned. I began to search for other Scriptures
that spoke of restoring or restoration. There were several.
Then I came upon one which spoke of the return of the
Lord in conjunction with the restoration of all things. It
was recorded in Acts. It is a wonderful verse, I thought,
that begins to put things together. I couldn't wait to share
it with Solomon. I rehearsed what I would say in my mind.
I would say, "Solomon listen to this: 'Repent therefore
and be converted, that your sins may be blotted out, so
that times of refreshing may come from the presence of
the Lord, and that He may send Jesus Christ, who was
preached to you before, whom heaven must receive until
the times of restoration of all things.' Do you hear that,
Solomon? It doesn't say 'until the restoration of all things,'
but 'until the *times of restoration.'* Are we in the times of

restoration, Solomon?" I continued rehearsing what I would say. "Add to that, Solomon, 'which God has spoken by the mouth of all His holy prophets since the world began.' That is the end of the passage."

Finally, the time came. Solomon was waiting in his study, and I approached with a grin on my face again. "I assume, by the smile on your face," he said, "you believe you have heard from our Lord once again, James."

"Absolutely, Solomon!" I said.

"You can rejoice in the Lord, but do not be smug about what you gain in your relationship with Him."

"I'm not being smug, Solomon. At least I don't think I am. I hope I'm not."

"It is just a warning, James. We must remain humble, especially if we are going to serve our Lord and His people. Every good and perfect gift comes from Him. We are not the author of truth. We are simply the bearers of truth, if indeed we have heard the truth from Him, and that is only determined through testing. Once again, James, it is not wrong to enter into supposition, which most often is where our search begins, however, we must seek to end in truth. We are told in the Bible that Elijah will come and so we must assume that this passage concerning his coming will be fulfilled through a single person. Some believe that the two witnesses in the street must be Enoch and Elijah because they did not face death but were taken up to heaven. The Scripture says that it is appointed for every man to be born and to die. We know that the two witnesses will be put to death and their bodies will lie in the street, thus fulfilling that Scripture concerning every man being appointed to be born and to die. Others believe that it will be Moses and Elijah. Either way, the indication is that Elijah will actually come preceding Christ as the Scripture says. It is not wrong to suppose that there would also be a calling upon the end-time church to operate in the spirit of Elijah in preparing the way for the return of the Lord. Such a task would establish that there is still today a prophetic voice in the church and within Judaism, calling to the people of God, which includes those who are direct descendants of Jacob and those who are grafted in. The call to both houses of Israel, I believe, James, would be the same. It is a call back to the true worship of God in spirit and truth."

"What about turning the hearts of the fathers back to the children and the hearts of the children back to the fathers, Solomon. Would that also be a part of the Elijah Task in our day?"

"Yes, James. You see, what seperates the two now is that Christians embrace Yeshua as the Messiah of Israel and Israel does not. Israel holds to the truth of the Torah, the law and Christians do not. Christians say we are no longer under the Torah, the law, the very instruction of God concerning the true worship of God. The puzzle must be made whole again, James."

"Solomon! You knew the meaning of the puzzle all along!?"

"No, James. I have grown to understand its meaning just as you have. As a matter of fact, the Lord has revealed more to you than to me. It was you who brought up the issue of the Elijah Task when the Lord spoke it to you. Then it was you to whom the Lord spoke of the issue of restoration. Those two key words have led us to this point in our discussion."

"Solomon, I think there are already those on both sides of the mountain who are engaged in that prophetic call to abstain from mixed worship. I have heard from those who have climbed higher and then returned, that higher up the mountain, nearer to the place formed for God's redeemed, they have heard much the same thing from those on your side of the mountain. On my side of the mountain, there are those who are embracing the Torah, and there are those on your side of the mountain accepting Messiah as their Savior. These are amazing times we are living in, Solomon. I am covered with goosebumps just talking about these things."

"Yes, James, the turning of the hearts of the fathers and the children would be a restoration of broken relationship. Think of the church and Israel coming together in Christ, the Living Torah. What I am about to say is what has caused a division between me and those in the valley. Even when I have pointed only to the Scriptures and not given any commentary on it, they are completely closed to what I am about to say to you.

The Scriptures make it perfectly clear that there is no salvation outside of Israel. It is through His covenant with Israel that the God of Israel offers salvation to the world, through the blood of the Lamb of God, the Lamb of the God of Israel. God never made a covenant of salvation with any other nation on the face of the earth. Every covenant He renewed, He renewed with Israel, including what is called the New Covenant. Open your Bible, James, while I read Jeremiah 31:31-33:

> Behold, the days are coming, says, the LORD, when I will make a new covenant with the house of Israel and with the house of Judah—not according to the covenant that I made with their fathers in the day that I took them by the hand to lead them out of the land of Egypt, My covenant which they broke, though I was a husband to them, says the LORD. But this is the covenant that I will make with the house of Israel after those days, says the LORD: I will put My law in their minds, and write it on their hearts; and I will be their God, and they shall be My people.

"This is the New Covenant proclaimed by the church. Who is this covenant made with, James?"

"It is obvious that it is made with Israel, Solomon. Now I understand why certain denominations within the church have been claiming to be the new Israel, and that Israel has been cast off in favor of the church—the 'new Israel'."

"That's right, James. Those who believe that misinterpretation are more than hesitant to hear this Elijah call to the church today. Such was the case with your friends within the camp. I fully understand it. As I said before I too was there in my refusal to see Yeshua as the Messiah of Israel."

"I remember a passage from Matthew," I chimed in. "It is the passage where Yeshua said that He was not sent except to the lost sheep of the house of Israel, meaning to those of the Northern Kingdom who were scattered into the nations of the world."

"Yes, James, and once again, they were scattered by the very hand of God. A judgment that fits right into His plan of salvation, until all Israel is saved, as the apostle Paul reminds us. Though He scattered them into the nations of the world where they would eventually lose their identity as His people, He still would not abandon them. Those from the house of Israel who were scattered into the nations forgot their heritage. They no longer walked in the ways of the God of Israel. They were integrated into the culture where they were scattered. Just as your ancestors came from France, Ireland, and other countries to America, they have forgotten the way of their ancestors and are now simply Americans. Yet the God of Israel promised that He would not forsake them completely and would one day regather them."

"Remind me, Solomon. How does He do this, if they no longer know Him as God, if they do not call upon His name, if they do not listen for His words, and if they do not look for His leading?"

"These who were scattered were those of whom Yeshua was speaking when He said that He was sent for the lost sheep of the house of Israel. The regathering would be through the apostles and the disciples going out into those nations with the gospel of salvation through Yeshua. It is the amazing plan of salvation."

"It's sad though, Solomon. The Southern Kingdom, Judah, those who are called Jews, had maintained their identity and held to the law and the prophets. However, they then added to the Torah, making it such a form of mixed worship that they could not even identify Yeshua as their Messiah. They continue to call on the only true God and yet they still expectantly await the Messiah promised to them.

CHAPTER 21

Fisher of Men

IT HAD BECOME ANOTHER wonderful session with Solomon. In fact, it was so good, that Solomon wanted to meet right after lunch the next day. That sounded great to me, until I remembered that it would mean less time for prayer and study beforehand. I thought about studying more that evening, but, I really wanted just to sit in the chair by the window and take it all in. After getting ready for bed, I turned on the small lamp by the chair, sat down, and closed my eyes to pray. I began by thanking the Lord once again for all He was revealing to us. Then, of course, I asked Him to continue to show us more of the meaning of the puzzle.

I woke up in the chair before dawn. It was a little chilly, which is probably why I woke up, so I quickly got into bed and fell back asleep. A short while later I woke to the smell of something cooking and quickly gave thanks for whatever it was. Not that there is anything wrong with fruit in the morning, I really like eggs and fried potatoes. Solomon could also make a great omelet.

After breakfast, as I was cleaning up, I asked Solomon if he was going to spend some time studying before our afternoon meeting.

"I'm just going to be pulling some things together, James. Before we move on with the puzzle, I wanted to explain something to you about the Jews. That's why I wanted to meet this afternoon, and then perhaps we can meet this evening as well. I'm not sure how much time we have left before we part company."

That statement certainly took me by surprise. So much so, I was at a loss for words. "Alright, Solomon," was all I could manage.

"You see, James, I believe the Lord has been equipping us for something that He is about to disclose to us through the full interpretation of the puzzle. Fear not, my son. Whatever He has for us, it will be to His glory and to our pleasure in serving Him. I believe He has destined that we, along with many others, are about to engage more fully in sanctifying His name in the earth."

I wasn't sure what that meant. Solomon then added.

"That simply means to lift up His mighty name, so it does not remain common. You see, James, to take His name in vain is to make His name, which is to be above every other name, common. It also means to use His holy name to curse others, which we hear so much in our day."

"I think I understand what you mean, Solomon. I'll see you in a few hours."

I was excited about the meeting after lunch, but a little confused about why we might talk about the Jews. We had been making such good progress understanding the puzzle. Oh well, it could be one of a thousand things, I thought. There's no use trying to figure out what he might want to tell me. I might as well just wait. After going outside, I began walking a little ways from the cabin. I could see the settlement off in the distance and began to reflect on some things. If my time here with Solomon was coming to an end, I wanted to be sure to stop at the settlement on my return to pursuing the high places. I wanted to share what the Lord had shown me during my time with Solomon. I had no doubt I could thereafter find my former companions and rejoin them. They advanced the mountain at a snail's pace, always stopping to discuss things. If they weren't discussing issues among the brethren, they were spending time in prayer and looking for agreement among them as to the Lord's will. It was a good practice. It's one that I was formerly taught, and in turn taught to them.

As I walked along, my foot kicked up something in the grass. I bent down and took hold of it. It was two sticks tied together with a piece of leather. I looked at it for a moment and just as I was about to throw it into the nearby woods, I was given another vision in my mind's eye. It was an inner vision from the Lord that just kind of dropped into my head. I saw a man taking two sticks and tying them together. When I paused to pay attention, the words came to me: "As for you, son of man, take a stick for yourself and write on it: 'For Judah and for the children of Israel, his companions.' Then take another stick and write on it, 'For Joseph, the stick of Ephraim, and for all the house of Israel, his companions.' Then join them one to another for yourself into one stick, and they will become one in your hand.'" It was Ezekiel 37! The passage concerning the dry bones and one kingdom, one King. I had memorized that passage years ago. I looked at the sticks in my hand again. There was nothing written on them, but they were certainly two sticks tied together. As I walked, I held onto the two sticks and began to pray. "Lord, I have never had a time in my life when you have spoken so much to me. These two sticks remind me of Ezekiel's visions. What are you preparing us for, Lord?"

Since we had eaten a fairly big breakfast, Solomon made some sandwiches to enjoy along with a few chips that his companions had delivered as a treat. After we ate, Solomon rose from the table and asked, "Are you finished, my son?"

"Yes," I said.

"Shall we go right into my study, and you can clean up after we talk?"

We entered his study, sat down, and Solomon began to pray. I bowed my head and listened to his prayer. He prayed that his words would be clear and then prayed that the Lord would bless our conversation. I added my amen and lifted my head.

"James, I told you that I wanted to talk with you about the Jews. I'm going to ask you to simply listen to me without interruption. Some of the questions you will have may be answered as I continue along. In that way there is no need to interrupt the flow of what I want to say. If you still have questions when I am finished, I'll try to answer them then. Do you understand what I mean, James?"

"Yes, I understand. I'm all ears, Solomon." Oh, there's another one of those looks! I repeated, "No, I am listening, Solomon. Really.

"Indeed!" he said. And then he began his discourse: "James, you may recall in the course of our conversations we talked about how, after King Solomon died, the kingdom of Israel split into two kingdoms: the Northern Kingdom, also known as Ephraim, and the Southern Kingdom, also known as Judah. They were named after the largest tribe in each kingdom. You will recall that the Northern Kingdom was dispersed into the nations of the world. We are told that they lost their identity. They were no longer called Ephraim, or the Northern Kingdom. They no longer practiced the religious form that would identify them as Israelites. They became completely integrated into the nations in which they were dispersed, so much so that only God knew who they were after a few generations.

"On the other hand, the Southern Kingdom continued to follow the Torah. They honored the Sabbath and continued on with the temple service. They knew who they were, and they were known as the Israelites or Hebrews. The word *Hebrew* comes from the Hebrew word *ivri,* meaning 'from the other side.' Abraham came to the Land of Canaan from Mesopotamia which was on the other side of the Euphrates, so that's why he was called a Hebrew.

"When the Israelites, the Southern Kingdom, returned from captivity in Babylon under the leadership of Ezra, 80 percent of the Israelites were of the tribe of Judah. Therefore, the land became known as Judea instead of Israel, and the inhabitants were called Judeans, which eventually translated to Jews.

"In AD 70, when the temple was destroyed by the Romans, these Jews were scattered into the nations of the world, just as the Northern Kingdom had been. Some were driven into other Middle Eastern nations while others entered European nations. Still, they continued to worship the God of Israel and did not lose their identity. Keeping their identity is why we have seen the persecution of the Jews through the ages. Then, once Israel was declared the Jewish State, those known as Jews began to return to their homeland of Israel.

"What we now have in the world are Jews, mostly from the Southern Kingdom, who are known by the world only as Jews. We also have those from the Northern Kingdom who have searched out their ancestry and are returning to Israel. These are called Jews, even though they are not from the Southern Kingdom. All who identify with Israel through their ancestry are now called Jews. However, there are also, in most of the nations of the world, Israelites from the Northern Kingdom who still do not know they are Israelites.

"Once Yeshua came as the Lamb of God to offer salvation to all mankind, two things were taking place. One, He said that He came to the Jew first and also to the Greek. A Gentile is one who is not a Jew, so Greeks would be included in that. He also said He had sheep who were not of that fold, meaning the Jews. He was referring to the Israelites who had been scattered. Though they had lost their identity, He still knew who they were and where they were. He speaks of them prophetically many times through the prophets, and He gave the Apostle Paul the special commission to the Gentiles. "Both the Jews and the lost Israelites from the Northern Kingdom, are direct descendants of Jacob, whose name was changed to Israel by God, and are therefore called Israelites. Paul speaks of these Israelites as the ones who must be grafted in.

"So now we have the three groups: the Jews who are also Israelites, the Israelites who are not Jews—who are not originally from the tribe of Judah nor from Judea—and the Gentiles. Since the tribal era ended during the second temple period, there is no longer a distinction. Today, if one were to trace their heritage back and find they are descended from one of the Northern Tribes, we would call them Jews. The Gentiles, however, were not descendants of Abraham, Isaac and Jacob and thus also had to be grafted into the vine as a wild olive branch.

"Why is this important, James? It is important because of what is happening on the mountain today and will continue to happen as all things are being restored. On my side of the mountain, there are those who, by the leading of the Holy Spirit, are recognizing Yeshua as the Messiah of Israel. They are called Messianic Jews. Then there are those on your side of the mountain who are being led by the Holy Spirit to return to the Hebraic Roots of Christianity and in doing so are recognizing that they are grafted in to Israel. They become descendants of Abraham through adoption. They are also called sons and daughters of the God of Israel. In John's gospel, he tells us that these who received Christ as Lord and Savior, were given the right to become children of God, who are born, not of blood nor of the will of the flesh nor of the will of man but of God. So they are born again into the kingdom of God, into Israel. Through faith in Yeshua the Messiah, they are adopted into the family of Abraham and are grafted into Israel. By some, these are called Hebrew Roots Christians.

"It is vitally important to note here, James, that those 'Jews' who embrace Yeshua as their Messiah do not leave Judaism. They are following the example of Yeshua as their Messiah to live as He lived, walking out biblical Judaism. On the other hand, those within Christianity who recognize that they are grafted into Israel and become Israelites are not Jews. They too are seeking to live as

Yeshua lived, walking out biblical Judaism.

"Today, both the different forms of Judaism and of Christianity must conform to biblical Judaism in order to be true followers of Christ. This is what I believe the Holy Spirit is doing on both sides of the mountain today."

Solomon paused. "Now, I have said what I have to say. Let's find the scriptural evidence for my declaration to you. Do you want to take a break here, James, so that you can refresh yourself and get a drink? You may want to go to your room and collect your pen and pad to take down the Scripture references and some notes."

"Alright, Solomon, I'll be back in about ten or fifteen minutes." It was not that I was totally unaware of what Solomon had just shared with me. He did put it all in a very orderly manner. There had been people with me during my climb who were following the Lord's leading but who didn't understand the way in which He was leading me. They remarked that we were trying to become Jews because we honored the seventh day as the Sabbath, and we also began to honor the feasts of the Lord. The Holy Spirit led us to discover in the Scriptures that they were not Jewish feasts but are called the feasts of the Lord, and they are for all believers in the God of Israel. According to Scripture, the feasts were to be honored throughout all generations. The reason for celebrating them is the prophetic nature of the feasts. What has been accomplished by God in His plan of salvation has all taken place as the fulfillment of the spring feasts. What is yet to take place concerning the restoration of all things is prophetically laid out in the fall feasts. Yeshua honored these feasts as our example, staying within biblical Judaism and honoring the Torah of God, which is the instruction for the way the people of God are to worship Him and walk before Him.

I returned to the study with pen in hand and sat waiting for Solomon to continue.

"Let's begin with Yeshua in the New Testament and unwrap something found in John chapter 10 verse 16 where He said: 'And other sheep I have which are not of this fold; them also I must bring, and they will hear My voice; and there will be one flock and one shepherd.' Of course, the one flock and one shepherd is the final outcome, and we will get to that later. This passage begs the questions though: How would they hear His voice? How would He regather them?

"Well, as we unwrap this, we find that He had declared through the prophet Jeremiah how He would accomplish this great regathering, this greater exodus out of the nations of the world:

> "Therefore behold, the days are coming," says the LORD, "that it shall no more be said, 'The LORD lives who brought up the children of Israel from the land of Egypt', but, 'The LORD lives who brought up the children of Israel from the land of the north and from all the lands where He had driven them.' For I will bring them back into their land which I

gave to their fathers. Behold, I will send for many
fishermen, says the LORD, and they shall fish them.
(Jeremiah 16:14-16)

"He had declared it through the prophet Jeremiah,
and He would bring it about beginning with a band of
twelve men. They would be sent out, first to the Jews and
then to the nations of the world as fishers of men with the
gospel of salvation through Jesus Christ. Then He said to
them, "Follow Me, and I will make you fishers of men""
(Matthew 4:19).

"The gospel of salvation would be preached to the
nations, including all those unknowingly from the house
of Israel who were now Frenchmen, Englishmen, Iranians,
Turks, Russians, and Chinese. All nationalities would
hear the gospel and would once again put their faith in
the God of Israel as Christians. Those who are physical
descendants of Jacob would be grafted into Israel while
those who were not physical descendants, who had heard
that gospel and accepted Yeshua as Lord and Savior, also
would be grafted into Israel. Salvation comes to us because
of the covenant with Israel. Romans 11 lays this out very
clearly. I encourage you to read and study that chapter,
James.

"Jeremiah, in declaring the Lord's intent, speaks
further on this subject. Following the fishers of men, the
Lord then says through the prophet that He will send out
hunters who will hunt them down from every mountain,

hill, and even from the crevices of the rocks. So, James, we have Scriptures from both the Old and New Testaments speaking to us of these events designed by God to bring His people back from both sides of the mountain. We are further told over and over again in the term 'day of the LORD' to identify the seventh day, the seventh one thousand years within the seven-thousand-year plan of salvation. Yeshua came to earth during the fifth day, the fifth one-thousand-year period. It has been slightly more than two thousand years since His coming, which closes out the fifth and sixth days. Since there is some debate about lost years within the biblical calendar, in which these dates are set, we cannot know or predict the day or the hour. However, Yeshua tells us that we are to know the season of His return through the signs given to us.

"Now, James, what we must do is take this information given to us in the Scriptures and pull together those passages concerning the day of the LORD. Then we must consider those other passages speaking of the end of kingdoms in the book of Daniel and seek to understand the book of Revelation in the light of these things. We also need to consider the completion of the feasts of the Lord, and what is prophetically spoken of especially within those fall feasts, which are not yet fulfilled.

"This is important, James. We must consider all these things, in light of the Elijah Task for the church and Israel and the puzzle. This, I believe, is the reason why you have been brought to my home, James. You have given prophetic insight through your gifting by the Holy Spirit, and the Lord has used my knowledge of Israel and the Scriptures so that we can each be used by the Lord to join those on both sides of the mountain who are now engaged in this Elijah Task. This task is calling His people out of mixed worship, to the true worship of the God of Israel, as a part of the fulfillment of Acts 3 concerning the time of the restoration of all things in order that Christ may come to establish His Kingdom upon the earth."

CHAPTER 22

Heading Down the Mountain?

SOLOMON HAD SUGGESTED THAT we take all the time we needed to finish our study and preparation. We chose to postpone our evening meetings until we felt we were both prepared, through prayer and study, to come back together. Several weeks passed. I had visited the stream several times and we continued on with our daily chores, but for the most part, Solomon was in his study and I in my bedroom.

We chatted during our meals giving updates on how we were coming along. Then finally one evening Solomon said, "I have just about completed my task, James. How are you coming along with yours?"

"I believe I have been able to put things together with a rather strong scriptural basis for my conclusions, Solomon."

"Then perhaps the hour has come, my son. My friends will be here on Thursday. That gives us two more days to complete a summary for us to share with them."

"What do you mean, Solomon? Do you mean we are going to combine what we have each concluded and share it with them for their judgment?"

"No, James, what I mean is that I will share my conclusion and then you will share your conclusion. We will ask them if they bear witness to what we believe God is speaking to us."

"Solomon, to be honest with you, I really don't like my conclusion, but there is no getting around what I believe the Lord is saying, or more aptly put, to that which the Lord is calling me."

"If my friends and I witness to it as being from the Lord, are you willing to accept that witness? Are you willing to be obedient to walk it out, to fulfill your calling?"

"Yes, I believe I am, Solomon. Otherwise what has this all been about?"

"Exactly, James. Exactly."

The two days passed quickly. I spent my time awaiting their arrival by praying, asking the Lord to help me put forth my conclusion with clarity, and that He would give me the courage to accept whatever the outcome. Solomon's friends may be hesitant in giving counsel over such matters. They probably think they're just coming with the supplies and for a visit. If that's the case, they are in for a big surprise.

After all the supplies had been put away, Solomon asked if we could all join him in his study. We grabbed two kitchen chairs. I put one next to Solomon's desk and gave the more comfortable chair to one of the guests. I thought the living room would have been more comfortable until I saw how many books Solomon had piled upon his desk. Wow! I thought, all I have is my Bible and a notepad. I hope he's going first.

Once we were seated, Solomon began. "My friends, this is a very special day for us all. James and I would like to share our journey with you. We'd like you to consider all we are going to share with you in the light of your years of studying the Scriptures, your relationship with Yeshua, and the gifting of His Holy Spirit. Will you join me in prayer to that end?"

Solomon's two friends began speaking to each other in Hebrew. I didn't know what they were saying, but at the end of their conversation, they agreed, bowed their heads, held their hands up above them and began to pray. I was surprised, because I thought Solomon was going to lead us in prayer. Solomon likewise bowed his head and lifted his hands, and so I did the same. The three of them began to all pray at the same time. I didn't pray. I listened to them praying for wisdom, discernment and blessing as well as for understanding and witness and for the Lord's will to be done. Then all stopped praying just about at the same moment.

Solomon lifted his head and said, "James, would you like to begin?" I didn't answer right away because I really didn't want to be the first. He then said, "Alright, James. I will begin."

"Thank you, Solomon," I said, as I sat back in my chair.

To my surprise, Solomon began by explaining what had happened when he used to visit with the others in the valley. He shared how well they got along, so long as things were left on a casual level. However, when they agreed to begin sharing the Scriptures together, he found that the invitations became less and less until they made it clear that they could not agree with his understanding of the Scriptures. They were concerned he would confuse the people whom they were pastoring. From there, he explained my arrival and his belief about what the plan of God was for us. He shared everything with them right up to the puzzle and the key words God had given us through our conversations. Then at the end of his two-hour-long discussion, stopping to answer their questions many times, he came to his conclusion. He said that he believed both he and I were to descend the mountain to share with all who would hear the call of the Elijah Task—the call to abandon mixed worship in preparation for the second coming of the Lord. He believed God was calling him to add his voice to those who were already speaking out on his side of the mountain and that God was calling me to do the same on my side of the mountain. He believed that this Elijah Task was indeed to be the prophetic voice of the redeemed calling all the children of God back to Him through His Word.

As he ended, Solomon asked if either of the two friends had any further questions for him. Neither of them did. Solomon then asked me if I would start by sharing with them about my pursuit up the mountain, which ultimately led me to his cabin. Once again, I was surprised by Solomon's request. However, I did as he asked by hitting on just the highlights of my pursuit up the mountain. I must say, it was good to go back and reflect on it all, and it was good to see that their reaction was so affirming.

Eventually, I finished, bringing us up to the present. Here were four men sitting and seeking the will of God, seeking a witness of two or three so that we could move forward with confidence. I awaited their response and was a little discouraged when I heard it. They wanted to take what we had shared with them back to the community of believers on their side of the mountain to pray with them and requested that we give them until they next brought supplies. They then would return with what they believed God wanted for both Solomon and me. Solomon quickly agreed with them. We stood to our feet, walked them out onto the porch, and said our goodbyes.

"Solomon, why did you agree so quickly with them and not ask what they were feeling about what we shared?"

"Well, James, I think what they want to do is wise. These are mature men of God who live in a very mature community of believers. They are not going to take what we have asked of them lightly. They know this has to do with our futures, and it is a lot to ask of them. I personally appreciate their great concern for you and me."

"I know you're right, Solomon. I'm a little anxious. Not just about what God has for us but about leaving here, especially about descending the mountain. I have spent years climbing to get this high. During my ascent things were getting pretty shaky on my side of the mountain. You talk about mixed worship. There were all kinds of worldly things coming into the church, and not a whole lot was being done about it."

"Perhaps things have gotten better in your absence, James. You know, God has a way of sweeping out His church. Usually through judgment."

"I know, Solomon. It all goes back to trusting in Him, doesn't it?"

CHAPTER 23

The Call

IT WAS ONLY TWO weeks, but it seemed like a lifetime before the day arrived for Solomon's friends to return with the supplies and with their word to us. It certainly wasn't as if everything rested on what they had to say. There were other factors to be considered as well. Spending those two weeks in prayer, a certain knowledge settled into me concerning what God would have me do. Granted, their witness to what I believed God had revealed for me would be great in settling the matter, but what would I do if they didn't agree with what I felt God was saying to me? Could I disregard what they present and do what I feel the Lord is telling me? That would be awkward, especially if Solomon agreed with them. Having these thoughts racing through my head was making me very anxious, so I stopped and dismissed those thoughts from my head and asked for the peace of the Lord to be brought to me by the Holy Spirit.

"James," Solomon called out. "Our guests have arrived. Could you come down and help with the supplies?"

"Coming." I responded.

After all the supplies were put away, in record time I might add, we all took our seats in the living room. Solomon asked if they would like something to drink. I thought to myself, oh Solomon, just let them start talking, will you?

"My brothers," said one of the men, I believe his name was Benjamin. We called each other "my friend" or "my brother" so often that I never could remember their names. I think he was Benjamin and the other Joshua. "We have spent much time in prayer before the Lord over the matter that you have asked us to consider. We believe the puzzle to be very significant. Among the twelve of us who have held this up before the Lord, there is no dissent among us. We are all in agreement. The Elijah Task is a corporate call on both sides of the mountain to prepare for the coming of the Lord. We also agree that it will be instrumental in bringing together both houses of Israel and therefore the restoration of the whole house of Israel. With one voice we concur that you both are to return to your side of the mountain and enter into this Elijah Task. We believe that you are to call for the abandonment of mixed worship. We believe that God will give you clear evidence of what such mixed worship is as you descend the mountain. We believe that God will join you with others who have this same calling, and you are to gather to yourself others willing to share in the task. Once you have reached the bottom, you will begin your ascent a second time. Only this time, your ascent will be during the beginning of the seventh day. As you know, the biblical day begins with darkness, known as the tribulation period. We are convinced our God will be in the process of leading His people on both sides of the mountain to the top, to the place that is formed for God's redeemed, to Jerusalem. It is during the second climb that the bride of Christ will prepare herself to be wed to her Groom, Yeshua."

Solomon stood up with his hands in the air and started dancing around the room singing something in Hebrew. I just sat in the chair with a grin on my face as I watched the other two men join him. When they had finished, we walked together out onto the porch and said our farewells. I knew there was a strong possibility that I would not see them again.

There were still a few hours before the sun would set, so I asked Solomon if he minded if I walked down to the stream. He said he didn't mind and that he would have dinner ready by the time I got back. I knew Solomon would ask me how I felt about the conclusion, and I wanted to prepare. After a couple hours, I returned to the house. At dinner, Solomon wasted no time. "James, how is all of this setting with you?"

"I'm feeling so many things right now, Solomon. I feel excited by the Lord's calling. I feel frightened about going it alone until the Lord brings others to me or me to others who are like-minded. I feel very sad at the thought of leaving you. I feel challenged, and ill equipped, and so many, many other things."

"I do as well, my son. And I too will miss you greatly. The Lord has made us soul mates James, and that does not happen often in this life. I will cherish this time we have had together as one of the treasures the Lord has given me in this life."

"I feel exactly the same way, Solomon."

We had a few more good weeks talking about where we would start and how we would start. We both knew the task was going to require the Lord's divine appointments. We simply had to continually look for them and recognize them as they came along. I told Solomon that my first stop would be the settlement down the valley a little way from the cabin. He agreed.

Sadly, the time had come. I stood with the few things I had brought with me to the cabin that first day. Solomon put his hands on my shoulders and just looked at me for a long moment. He then kissed me on both checks, and said,

"Y'va-reh-ch'cha Adonai v'yeesh-m'reh'cha,
Ya-air Adonai pa-nahv ay-leh-cha vee-choo-neh-ka,
Yee-sa Adonai pa-nahv ay-leh-cha v'ya-same l'cha
Shalom.

May the Lord bless you and watch over you;
May the Lord shine His face upon you
and be gracious to you;
May the Lord manifest His presence to you
and establish you in peace."

With that we parted.

Scripture References

Chapter 2 The Divine Appointment
Romans 1:20
Acts 9:15
Hebrews 4:12
Deuteronomy 19:15

Chapter 3 The Settlement
Isaiah 28:10
Hebrews 6:1-3

Chapter 5 The Holy Conversation/It's A Matter of History
2 Samuel 5:7
Psalm 97:8
Isaiah 8:18
Amos 1:2
Psalm 48:2-3
Isaiah 33:5; 28:16; 35:10; 51:11; 30:19; 2:3
Micah 4:2
Zechariah 8:3
Isaiah 59:20

Mark 9:35
Acts 17:11

Chapter 6 The Holy Conversation/What about Tradition
Isaiah 60: 1-3
Amos 3:3
1 Kings 11
1 Chronicles 5:26
1 Chronicles 10
Deuteronomy 28:64
2 Kings 25
Matthew 28:16-20
Matthew 10:5-6
Matthew 15:24
Jeremiah 16:16
John 8:32

Chapter 7 The Gospel of Salvation
John 3:16
Galatians 1:8
2 Corinthians 5:20
1 Corinthians 2:14-15
Romans 3:1-2
Matthew 28:18-20

Chapter 8 Back to the Stream
Isaiah 49:10
Zechariah 4:10

Romans 8:29
Genesis 25:19-34; 27:1-40

Chapter 9 The Gospel of the Kingdom
Genesis 17:5
John 8:39
Genesis 12:1-3, 7
Genesis 13:14-17
Genesis 15:1-22
Genesis 22:15-18
Matthew 15:24
Revelation 5:5
Jeremiah 31:31-34
Romans 11
Ephesians 2:11-22
John 1: 13
Romans 11:26
Isaiah 27:9

Chapter 10 Honoring the Sabbath
John 14:15
1 John 2:6
Matthew 10:24
Deuteronomy 4:2
Deuteronomy 12:32
Exodus 20:8
Leviticus 23:3
Genesis 2:2

Genesis 2:3
Mark 2:27
Genesis 1:2
Genesis 1:5

Chapter 11 The Seven Thousand Year Plan
Ephesians 1:4
Psalm 90:4
2 Peter 3:8
Matthew 24

Chapter 12 The Mission of Yeshua
Isaiah 6:1-3
Genesis 17:7
Jeremiah 31:31-33
Genesis 32:28
1 Chronicles 2:1
Genesis 48
Genesis 3:16-19
Deuteronomy 6:4
John 17:11
Isaiah 42:6
Isaiah 40-55
John 1:1-3
John 5:43
John 6:38
Matthew 5:17-20
Ezekiel 34:11-12

Chapter 13 The Lord is my Shepherd
Psalm 23
John 17:6

Chapter 14 The Visit
Psalm 23
Hebrews 4:12

Chapter 15 Home Again
Matthew 6: 25-34

Chapter 16 The Law
2 Timothy 3:16-17
2 Peter 1:20
Ezekiel 47
Revelation 22:1
Isaiah 59:2
1 John 3:4
1 John 1:7
1 John 2:6
Deuteronomy 8:3
Matthew 4:4
John 17:8
John 16:13
John 1:7
Jeremiah 23:1
Ezekiel 34
James 3:1

Chapter 17 The Puzzle
Genesis 1:1-2:1
Genesis 2:15
Genesis 7:1-8:1
Genesis 22:10
Genesis 24:1-50:26
Exodus 3:7
Exodus 32:15
Exodus 40:34
1 Samuel 10:1
1 Samuel 17:50
1 Kings 11:41-43
1 Kings 12
2 Kings 17
Daniel 9
Mark 16:1-8
Revelation 21-22
Romans 11:17-24
Ephesians 2:11-23

Chapter 18 The Elijah Task/History Speaking
1 Kings 17-19
Matthew 11:14
1 Kings 11-14
1 Kings 16:31-33
1 Kings 17
1 Kings 18:21
Malachi 4:4-6

Chapter 19 The Spirit and the Power of Elijah
Matthew 17:11-13
Luke 1:13-17
Joel 2:10-11
Zephaniah 1:14
1 John 2:11
Matthew 23:4-5, 11
Matthew 5:17-18

Chapter 20 The Restoration
Ezra 6:1-11
Acts 3:19-21
Hebrews 9:27
Jeremiah 31:31-33

Chapter 21 Fishers of Men
Ezekiel 37:15-17
Matthew 24:2
Mark 13:2
Genesis 11: 27-32
Romans 1:16
Genesis 35:10
Romans 11
John 1:12-13
John 10:16
Jeremiah 16:14-16
Matthew 4:19

Chapter 23 The Call
Numbers 6:22-27

Bibliography

R. LAIRD Harris, Gleason L. Archer, Jr. Bruce K. Waltke, *Theological Wordbook of the Old Testament* (Chicago: Moody Press, 2003), entry #1910.

Restoration Scriptures True Name Edition Study Bible, Third Edition: (MacClenny, FL: YATI Publishing, 2007).

Destiny Seekers, Look Higher Than the Mountain by James E. Morel

CPSIA information can be obtained
at www.ICGtesting.com
Printed in the USA
LVHW042008070219
606816LV00001B/11/P